Artificial Intelligence for Humans, Volume 2: Nature-Inspired Algorithms

Artificial Intelligence for Humans, Volume 2: Nature-Inspired Algorithms

Jeff Heaton

Heaton Research, Inc.
St. Louis, MO, USA

Publisher: Heaton Research, Inc.
Artificial Intelligence for Humans, Volume 2: Nature-Inspired Algorithms
August, 2014
Author: Jeff Heaton
Editor: Tracy Heaton
Technical Editor: Aaron Basil (Ethervision)
ISBN: 978-1499720570
Edition: 1.0

Copyright ©2014 by Heaton Research Inc., 1734 Clarkson Rd. #107, Chesterfield, MO 63017-4976. World rights reserved. The author(s) created reusable code in this publication expressly for reuse by readers. Heaton Research, Inc. grants readers permission to reuse the code found in this publication or downloaded from our website so long as (author(s)) are attributed in any application containing the reusable code and the source code itself is never redistributed, posted online by electronic transmission, sold or commercially exploited as a stand-alone product. Aside from this specific exception concerning reusable code, no part of this publication may be stored in a retrieval system, transmitted, or reproduced in any way, including, but not limited to photo copy, photograph, magnetic, or other record, without prior agreement and written permission of the publisher.

Heaton Research, Encog, the Encog Logo and the Heaton Research logo are all trademarks of Heaton Research, Inc., in the United States and/or other countries.

TRADEMARKS: Heaton Research has attempted throughout this book to distinguish proprietary trademarks from descriptive terms by following the capitalization style used by the manufacturer.

The author and publisher have made their best efforts to prepare this book, so the content is based upon the final release of software whenever possible. Portions of the manuscript may be based upon pre-release versions supplied by software manufacturer(s). The author and the publisher make no representation or warranties of any kind with regard to the completeness or accuracy of the contents herein and accept no liability of any kind including but not limited to performance, merchantability, fitness for any particular purpose, or any losses or damages of any kind caused or alleged to be caused directly or indirectly from this book.

SOFTWARE LICENSE AGREEMENT: TERMS AND CONDITIONS

The media and/or any online materials accompanying this book that are available now or in the future contain programs and/or text files (the "Software") to be used in connection with the book. Heaton Research, Inc. hereby grants to you a license to use and distribute software programs that make use of the compiled binary form of this book's source code. You may not redistribute the source code contained in this book, without the written permission of Heaton Research, Inc. Your purchase, acceptance, or use of the Software will constitute your acceptance of such terms.

The Software compilation is the property of Heaton Research, Inc. unless otherwise indicated and is protected by copyright to Heaton Research, Inc. or other copyright owner(s) as indicated in the media files (the "Owner(s)"). You are hereby granted a license to use and distribute the Software for your personal, noncommercial use only. You may not reproduce, sell, distribute, publish, circulate, or commercially exploit the Software, or any portion thereof, without the written consent of Heaton Research, Inc. and the specific copyright owner(s) of any component software included on this media.

In the event that the Software or components include specific license requirements or end-user agreements, statements of condition, disclaimers, limitations or warranties ("End-User License"), those End-User Licenses supersede the terms and conditions herein as to that particular Software component. Your purchase, acceptance, or use of the Software will constitute your acceptance of such End-User Licenses.

By purchase, use or acceptance of the Software you further agree to comply with all export laws and regulations of the United States as such laws and regulations may exist from time to time.

SOFTWARE SUPPORT

Components of the supplemental Software and any offers associated with them may be supported by the specific Owner(s) of that material but they are not supported by Heaton Research, Inc.. Information regarding any available support may be obtained from the Owner(s) using the information provided in the appropriate README files or listed elsewhere on the media.

Should the manufacturer(s) or other Owner(s) cease to offer support or decline to honor any offer, Heaton Research, Inc. bears no responsibility. This notice concerning support for the Software is provided for your information only. Heaton Research, Inc. is not the agent or principal of the Owner(s), and Heaton Research, Inc. is in no way responsible for providing any support for the Software, nor is it liable or responsible for any support provided, or not provided, by the Owner(s).

WARRANTY

Heaton Research, Inc. warrants the enclosed media to be free of physical defects for a period of ninety (90) days after purchase. The Software is not available from Heaton Research, Inc. in any other form or media than that enclosed herein or posted to www.heatonresearch.com. If you discover a defect in the media during this warranty period, you may obtain a replacement of identical format at no charge by sending the defective media, postage prepaid, with proof of purchase to:

Heaton Research, Inc.
Customer Support Department
1734 Clarkson Rd #107
Chesterfield, MO 63017-4976
Web: www.heatonresearch.com
E-Mail: support@heatonresearch.com

DISCLAIMER

Heaton Research, Inc. makes no warranty or representation, either expressed or implied, with respect to the Software or its contents, quality, performance, merchantability, or fitness for a particular purpose. In no event will Heaton Research, Inc., its distributors, or dealers be liable to you or any other party for direct, indirect, special, incidental, consequential, or other damages arising out of the use of or inability to use the Software or its contents even if advised of the possibility of such damage. In the event that the Software includes an online update feature, Heaton Research, Inc. further disclaims any obligation to provide this feature for any specific duration other than the initial posting.

The exclusion of implied warranties is not permitted by some states. Therefore, the above exclusion may not apply to you. This warranty provides you with specific legal rights; there may be other rights that you may have that vary from state to state. The pricing of the book with the Software by Heaton Research, Inc. reflects the allocation of risk and limitations on liability contained in this agreement of Terms and Conditions.

SHAREWARE DISTRIBUTION

This Software may use various programs and libraries that are distributed as shareware. Copyright laws apply to both shareware and ordinary commercial software, and the copyright Owner(s) retains all rights. If you try a shareware program and continue using it, you are expected to register it. Individual programs differ on details of trial periods, registration, and payment. Please observe the requirements stated in appropriate files.

This book is dedicated to my wonderful wife, Tracy, and our cockatiels, Cricket and Wynton.

Contents

Forward		xvii
Introduction		xxi
0.1	Series Introduction	xxi
	0.1.1 Programming Languages	xxii
	0.1.2 Online Labs	xxiii
	0.1.3 Code Repositories	xxiii
	0.1.4 Books Planned for the Series	xxiv
	0.1.5 Other Resources	xxiv
0.2	Nature-Inspired Algorithms Introduction	xxv
0.3	Structure of this Book	xxvi
0.4	The Kickstarter Campaign	xxvii
0.5	Background Information	xxix
	0.5.1 Vectors	xxix
	0.5.2 Distance	xxxi
	0.5.3 Modeling with an RBF Network	xxxiii
	0.5.4 Radial-Basis Functions	xxxiv
	0.5.5 Radial-Basis Function Networks	xxxvi
1 Population, Scoring, and Selection		**1**
1.1	Understanding Populations	3

		1.1.1	Initial Population	4
		1.1.2	Competition Among Population Members	5
		1.1.3	Cooperation Among Population Members	5
		1.1.4	Phenotype and Genotype	6
		1.1.5	Populations on Islands	7
	1.2	Scoring Populations		8
	1.3	Selecting from Populations		8
	1.4	Truncation Selection		9
	1.5	Tournament Selection		11
	1.6	How to Choose Round Count		14
	1.7	Fitness-Proportionate Selection		15
	1.8	Stochastic Universal Sampling		17
		1.8.1	Choosing a Selection Algorithm	19
	1.9	Chapter Summary		20

2 Crossover and Mutation — 23

	2.1	Evolutionary Algorithms		24
	2.2	Solution Encoding		26
	2.3	Mutation		27
		2.3.1	Shuffle Mutation	28
		2.3.2	Perturb Mutation	29
	2.4	Crossover		31
		2.4.1	Splice Crossover	32
		2.4.2	No Repeat Splice Crossover	34
		2.4.3	Other Mutation and Crossover Strategies	36
	2.5	Why is Elitism Necessary?		37
	2.6	Chapter Summary		38

3 Genetic Algorithms — 41

	3.1	Genetic Algorithms for Discrete Problems	42
		3.1.1 The Traveling Salesman Problem (TSP)	42
		3.1.2 Designing a Genetic Algorithm for the TSP	45
		3.1.3 Application of the TSP to a Genetic Algorithm	47
	3.2	Genetic Algorithms for Continuous Problems	49
	3.3	Other Applications of Genetic Algorithms	52
		3.3.1 Tag Clouds	52
		3.3.2 Mosaic Art	54
	3.4	Chapter Summary	56
4	**Genetic Programming**		**59**
	4.1	Programs as Trees	60
		4.1.1 Postfix Notation	62
		4.1.2 Tree Notation	63
		4.1.3 Terminal and Non-terminal Nodes	65
		4.1.4 Evaluating Trees	66
		4.1.5 Generating Trees	68
		4.1.6 Full Tree Initialization	69
		4.1.7 Grow Tree Initialization	71
		4.1.8 Ramped Half-and-Half Initialization	73
		4.1.9 Reservoir Sampling	73
	4.2	Mutating Trees	77
	4.3	Tree Crossover	79
	4.4	Fitting Equations	81
	4.5	Chapter Summary	84
5	**Speciation**		**87**
	5.1	Speciation Implementations	88
		5.1.1 Threshold Speciation	88

		5.1.2 Clustering Speciation	89
	5.2	Speciation in Genetic Algorithms	91
	5.3	Speciation in Genetic Programming	92
	5.4	Using Speciation	93
	5.5	Chapter Summary	94

6 Particle Swarm Optimization   97

	6.1	Flocking	98
	6.2	Particle Swarm Optimization	101
		6.2.1 Particles	102
		6.2.2 Velocity Calculation	103
		6.2.3 Implementation	104
	6.3	Chapter Summary	107

7 Ant Colony Optimization   109

	7.1	Discrete Ant Colony Optimization	111
		7.1.1 ACO Initialization	113
		7.1.2 Ant Movement	114
		7.1.3 Pheromone Update	118
	7.2	Continuous Ant Colony Optimization	120
		7.2.1 Initial Candidate Solutions	122
		7.2.2 Ant Movement	123
	7.3	Chapter Summary	126

8 Cellular Automata   129

	8.1	Elementary Cellular Automation	130
	8.2	Conway's Game of Life	135
		8.2.1 Rules of the Game of Life	137
		8.2.2 Interesting Life Patterns	138
	8.3	Evolve your Own Cellular Automata	141

8.3.1 Understanding Merge Physics	145
8.4 Chapter Summary	149

9 Artificial Life — 151

- 9.1 Milestone 1: Drawing a Plant 153
- 9.2 Milestone 2: Animating Plant Growth 157
  - 9.2.1 Plant Physics 158
  - 9.2.2 Plant Growth 162
- 9.3 Milestone 3: Evolving a Plant 164
  - 9.3.1 Scoring a Plant 166
- 9.4 Chapter Summary 166

10 Modeling — 169

- 10.1 Competitive Data Science 171
- 10.2 Milestone 1: Wrangling the Data 174
- 10.3 Milestone 2: Build a Model 178
- 10.4 Milestone 3: Submit a Test Response 181
- 10.5 Chapter Summary 183

A Examples — 185

- A.1 Artificial Intelligence for Humans 185
- A.2 Staying Up to Date 186
- A.3 Obtaining the Examples 186
  - A.3.1 Download ZIP File 186
  - A.3.2 Clone the Git Repository 187
- A.4 Example Contents 188
- A.5 Contributing to the Project 191

References — 193

Forward

by Dave Snell, ASA, MAAA, FLMI, CLU, ChFC, ARA, ACS, MCP
Technology evangelist, RGA Reinsurance Company

As editor for several years of the Society of Actuaries' *Forecasting & Futurism* newsletter, I have had the pleasure of working with many talented mathematicians, economists, and futurists who are sharing their knowledge about new techniques to better deal with our increasingly complex world. A couple of years ago, I persuaded Jeff Heaton, a non-actuary, to enter our genetic algorithms contest, and he won it! Jeff has since been a frequent contributor, a colleague (we now work together), a co-presenter at Society of Actuaries meetings across the country, and a great friend and co-conspirator in our ongoing adventure into machine learning. Jeff has been involved in machine learning, artificial intelligence (AI), and associated topics for a long time. It was his hobby and a passion for him; now he is employed as a data scientist and loving the chance to indulge in his hobby on the day job. His enthusiasm is contagious, and I think you will discover that as you read his books.

Jeff's website, www.heatonresearch.com gets over 100,000 hits per month from researchers, academics, and just plain hobbyists across the world. ENCOG, his open source engine for cognitive studies, is used by medical doctors looking for better ways to detect cancers and high frequency traders trying to optimize their trade algorithms.

Recently, Jeff was accepted into a PhD program in computer science. Unlike several other AI book authors, Jeff is not an academic professor trying to pontificate and obfuscate with sophisticated formulas and arcane terminologies to flaunt his intellectual prowess. Some of those books seem self-serving and tiresome. Likewise, he is not assuming that the reader is a "dummy." I personally find the Dummies series of books objectionable. Who wants to be treated as a dummy? Jeff is one of us! He has learned his craft by reading and doing and coding and revising. He struggled with the linear algebra necessary for some AI solutions and had to take courses to learn it. He has empathy for the intelligent layperson who wants to learn about AI and needs some help through the specialized mathematics. He spares us the learning curve of a favorite programming language that some author decides to impose upon all readers. Jeff has made a special effort to make this book readable by humans - not dummies - not just PhDs in statistics or computer science. It is for real humans who want to understand what this AI stuff is all about and why it is taking on ever increasing importance as the big data tsunami engulfs us.

Jeff has learned from feedback on his ENCOG engine and on his previous books that a reader does not want to have to learn a new computer programming language just to try a new AI technique. The examples here are in pseudocode so that everyone can understand them; the website provides them in several programming languages for you so you can reinforce the learning process with hands-on practice. You can make your own modifications to the "non-secret" code. This is not a black box type of presentation. It is an inducement to dive in and enjoy the pool! If you are a programmer in any of the languages Java, R, Python, C#, C, Scala, and probably lots more since this foreword was written, then you can download and run all of the examples. The code has been tested. It runs. You won't have to spend your time cursing the code instead of enjoying the AI learning experience.

OK, I emphasized how readable the book is. That does not mean it is trivial in content. In this volume, he covers topics such as genetic algorithms, ant colony optimization, and particle swarm optimization. He shows what they are, when and why they are useful, and how you can implement them. These are not trivial topics. His entire series *Artificial Intelligence for Humans* covers some exciting topics that most people consider daunting. Is it brain surgery? No! But it's neural networks and some leading-edge topics such as deep belief networks. Enjoy the book. Enjoy the series. Enjoy the adventure!

Dave Snell took early retirement in 2007 from his position as VP, Asia-Pacific Technology for RGA Reinsurance Company, where, based in Sydney, Australia, he managed new and existing technology for all of Asia and Australia. Currently, he is back home in the U.S. and a consultant to the Vice Chair of RGA, where he networks with kindred spirits among actuaries and technology associates to identify and overcome business obstacles through better use of technology tools. Dave has written thousands of programs in dozens of programming languages - including an artificial intelligence-based expert system in use in over a dozen countries and several languages. A machine learning process he co-invented was recently granted U.S. patent 8775218.

Introduction

- Series Introduction
- Example Computer Languages
- Prerequisite Knowledge
- Fundamental Algorithms
- Other Resources
- Structure of this Book

This book is the second in a series covering select topics in artificial intelligence (AI), a large field of study that encompasses many sub-disciplines. This introduction will provide some background information for readers who might not have read Volume 1. It is not necessary to read Volume 1 before this book. The following sections introduce both the series and the first volume.

0.1 Series Introduction

This series of books introduces the reader to a variety of popular topics in artificial intelligence. By no means are these volumes intended to be an exhaustive AI resource. However, each book presents a specific area of AI to familiarize the reader with some of the latest techniques in this field of computer science.

The series teaches artificial intelligence concepts in a mathematically gentle manner, which is why I named the series *Artificial Intelligence for Humans*. As a result, I always follow the theories with real-world programming examples and pseudocode instead of relying solely on mathematical formulas. Still, I make these assumptions:

- The reader is proficient in at least one programming language.

- The reader has a basic understanding of college algebra.

- The reader does not necessarily have much experience with formulas from calculus, linear algebra, differential equations, and statistics. I will introduce these formulas when necessary.

Finally, the book's examples have been ported to a number of programming languages. Readers can adapt the examples to the language that fits their particular programming needs.

0.1.1 Programming Languages

Although the book's text stays at the pseudocode level, I provide example packs for Java, C# and Python. The Scala programming language has a community-supplied port, and readers are also working on porting the examples to additional languages. So, your favorite language might have been ported since this printing. Check the book's GitHub repository for more information. I highly encourage readers of the books to help port to other languages. If you would like to get involved, Appendix A has more information to get you started.

0.1.2 Online Labs

Many of the examples from this series use JavaScript and are available to run online, using HTML5. Mobile devices must also have HTML5 capability to run the programs. You can find all online lab materials at the following web site:

http://www.aifh.org

These online labs allow you to experiment with the examples even as you read the e-book from a mobile device.

0.1.3 Code Repositories

All of the code for this project is released under the Apache Open Source License v2 and can be found at the following GitHub repository:

https://github.com/jeffheaton/aifh

The online labs, written in Javascript, can be found at the following GitHub repository:

https://github.com/jeffheaton/aifh-html

If you find something broken, misspelled, or otherwise botched as you work with the examples, you can fork the project and push a commit revision to GitHub. You will also receive credit among the growing number of contributors. Refer to Appendix A for more information on contributing code.

0.1.4 Books Planned for the Series

The following volumes are planned for this series:

- Volume 0: Introduction to the Math of AI
- Volume 1: Fundamental Algorithms
- Volume 2: Nature-Inspired Algorithms
- Volume 3: Deep Belief and Neural Networks

I will produce Volumes 1, 2, and 3 in order. Volume 0 is a planned prequel that I will create near the end of the series. While all the books will include the required mathematical formulas to implement the programs, the prequel will recap and expand on all the concepts from the earlier volumes. I also intend to produce more books on AI after the publication of Volume 3.

In general, you can read the books in any order. Each book's introduction will provide some background material from previous volumes. This organization allows you to jump quickly to the volume that contains your area of interest. If you want to supplement your knowledge at a later point, you can read the previous volume.

0.1.5 Other Resources

Many other resources on the Internet will be very useful as you read through this series of books.

The first resource is Khan Academy, a nonprofit educational website that provides videos to demonstrate many areas of mathematics. If you need additional review on any mathematical concept in this book, Khan Academy probably has a video on that information.

http://www.khanacademy.org/

The second resource is the Neural Network FAQ. This text-only resource has a great deal of information on neural networks and other AI topics.

http://www.faqs.org/faqs/ai-faq/neural-nets/

Although the information in this book is not necessarily tied to Encog, the Encog wiki has a fair amount of general information on machine learning.

http://www.heatonresearch.com/wiki/Main_Page

Finally, you can discuss AI and neural networks on the Encog forums. Since these forums are fairly active, community members or I will answer your questions.

http://www.heatonresearch.com/forum

0.2 Nature-Inspired Algorithms Introduction

Nature can inspire the artificial intelligence programmer. This book introduces algorithms based on genomes, birds, ants, and trees. These algorithms can be used to find optimal paths, recognize patterns, find equations behind data, and even simulate simple life.

Sometimes organisms in nature cooperate with each other. Packs of wolves will hunt together. Flocks of birds migrate together. As a programmer, you can design a group of virtual organisms to solve a problem together.

Other times, organisms in nature compete against each other. We can use survival of the fittest to guide the evolution of a program. Evolutionary algorithms allow multiple, potential solutions to compete, breed, and evolve. After many generations, a potentially good solution will evolve.

It is important to remember that we only seek inspiration from nature. We do not seek to duplicate nature. However, we can deviate from the biological processes should the need arise. Real biological processes are usually much more complex than the processes that even our most advanced computers can simulate.

0.3 Structure of this Book

Chapter 1, "Population and Scoring," introduces concepts that will be featured throughout the rest of the book. Nature-inspired algorithms solve problems by developing a population of solutions. Scoring allows the algorithm to evaluate the effectiveness of the members of a population.

Chapter 2, "Crossover and Mutation," shows several ways that population members can create potentially better solutions for the next generation. Crossover permits two or more potential solutions to combine their traits to create offspring for the next generation. Mutation lets a single genome create a slightly altered version of itself for the next generation.

Chapter 3, "Genetic Algorithms," combines the ideas from the previous chapters into a concrete algorithm. Genetic algorithms optimize fixed-length arrays through evolution to provide better results. This chapter will show how to use fixed-length arrays to find solutions for the traveling salesman problem (TSP) as well as to predict iris species using measurements of the flower.

Chapter 4, "Genetic Programming," demonstrates that the solution array for an evolutionary algorithm does not always need to be a fixed length. In fact, using these ideas, you can represent computer programs as trees that evolve to produce other programs that better perform their intended task.

Chapter 5, "Speciation," discusses how to divide the population into several different species. Just as crossover created offspring through the combination of two individuals from the population, speciation produces offspring through the mating of similar solutions. Programmers borrowed this concept from nature; only organisms of the same species pair off and reproduce.

Chapter 6, "Particle Swarm Optimization," uses groups of particles to search for optimal solutions. This grouping instinct in computer software is modeled after nature. Examples like herds of cattle, swarms of insects, flocks of birds, and schools of fish show the natural preference of organisms to travel in groups as the best solution against predators.

Chapter 7, "Ant Colony Optimization," discusses how the pheromone trails from ants can provide inspiration to computer programmers. As more ants follow the chemicals left by their fellow workers, the trails become stronger. Computer programs can incorporate a similar technique to find an optimal solution.

Chapter 8, "Cellular Automation," utilizes simple rules to produce very complex results and patterns. The key to creating an interesting cellular automation is to find simple rules that can be evolved using a human-based genetic algorithm.

Chapter 9, "Artificial Life," seeks to mirror life and contains one of the book's capstone projects. You will create a program that simulates the growth of plants. To help you check your progress, I will provide the code at three milestones.

Chapter 10, "Modeling Problems," discusses how data science uses nature-inspired algorithms. It also contains the book's second capstone project. Using data sets from one of the Kaggle (http://www.kaggle.com) tutorial competitions, I will show you how to create a model to predict whether the passengers on the Titanic survived or died. I also present this capstone in three milestones so that you can verify your progress.

0.4 The Kickstarter Campaign

In 2013, I launched this series of books after a successful Kickstarter campaign. Figure 1 shows the home page of the Kickstarter project for Volume 2.

Figure 1: The Kickstarter Campaign

You can visit the original Kickstarter at the following link:

http://goo.gl/kESfwp

I would like to thank all of the Kickstarter backers of the project. Without your support, this series might not exist. I would also like to extend a special thanks to those backers who supported the book at the $100 and higher levels. They are listed here in the order that they backed.

- Tracy Heaton (#1, repeat backer)
- Dr. Warren D. Lerner (#9, repeat backer)
- Travis Thaxton (#11, repeat backer)
- Steffen Andersen (#118, repeat backer)
- Dave Snell (#127, repeat backer)
- Jacob Kenner (#134)
- Jeffrey F. Elrod (#146, repeat backer)

- Damien Lebreuilly (#220, repeat backer)
- Peter Edwards (#242)
- Jeremy Achin (#325)
- Sergio Mendoza (#348)
- Dr. JT Kostman (#376)

Finally, I would like to give a very big thank you to Rory Graves and Matic Potocnik for porting the examples to Scala for both volumes. Aaron Basil (Ethervision) provided technical editing and valuable suggestions. My wife, Tracy Heaton, edited the book. Dave Snell provided advice and wrote the book's forward. Dan Walker also provided several great suggestions for the book.

Thank you, everyone–you are the best!

0.5 Background Information

You can read *Artificial Intelligence for Humans* in any order. However, this book does expand on some topics introduced in Volume 1. The next few sections will review these topics.

0.5.1 Vectors

A vector is essentially a one-dimensional array. Do not confuse the dimensionality of the vector array with the dimensions of your problem. Even if your problem had 10 inputs, you would still have a vector. Your 10 inputs would be stored in a vector of length 10.

In AI, a programmer uses a vector to store observations about a particular instance that might be a location, statistics on customers, measurements of a plant or even the weights of a neural network–it all depends on the problem you seek to solve. The idea of a vector connects to the real world concept of distance. For example, a point on a sheet of paper has two dimensions, which we usually call x and y. Likewise, a point in 3D space has three dimensions, with the labels as x, y, and z. You can store a two-dimensional point in a vector of length 2. Likewise, you can store a 3D point in a vector of length 3.

Although scientists sometimes consider time the fourth dimension, our universe comprises three perceivable dimensions. Adding time results in a manifold, or combination, but this does not imply that it is a true dimension compared with the other three. The combination of time with the three spatial dimensions is called the space-time continuum. Because humans cannot perceive these higher dimensions, comprehending dimensional spaces higher than three is difficult. However, high dimensional spaces are quite common in AI.

Because AI frequently uses the iris data set (Fisher, 1936), you will see it several times in this book. It contains measurements and species information for 150 iris flowers, and the data are essentially represented as a spreadsheet with the following columns or features:

- Sepal length
- Sepal width
- Petal length
- Petal width
- Iris species

Petals refer to the innermost petals of the iris, and sepal refers to the outermost petals of the iris flower. Even though the data set seems to have a vector of length 5, the species feature must be handled differently than the other four. In other words, vectors typically contain only numbers. So, the first four features are inherently numerical. The species feature is not.

One of the primary applications of this data set is to create a program that will act as a classifier. That is, it will consider the flower's features as inputs (sepal length, petal width, etc.,) and ultimately determine the species. This classification would be trivial for a complete and known data set, but our goal

0.5 Background Information

is to see whether the model can correctly identify the species using data from unknown irises.

Only simple numeric encoding translates the iris species to a single dimension. We must use additional dimensional encodings, such as one-of-n or equilateral, so that the species encodings are equidistant from each other. If we are classifying irises, we do not want our encoding process to create any biases.

Thinking of the iris features as dimensions in a higher dimensional space makes a great deal of sense. Consider the individual samples (the rows in the iris data set) as points in this search space. Points closer together likely share similarities. Let's take a look at these similarities by studying the following three rows from the iris data set:

```
5.1,3.5,1.4,0.2,Iris-setosa
7.0,3.2,4.7,1.4,Iris-versicolor
6.3,3.3,6.0,2.5,Iris-virginica
```

The first line has 5.1 as the sepal length, 3.5 as the sepal width, 1.4 as the petal length, and 0.2 as the petal width. If we use one-of-n encoding to the range 0 to 1, the above three rows would encode to the following three vectors:

```
[5.1,3.5,1.4,0.2,1,0,0]
[7.0,3.2,4.7,1.4,0,1,0]
[6.3,3.3,6.0,2.5,0,0,1]
```

Equilateral, discussed in Volume 1, is another way the species could have potentially been encoded. Now that you have the data in vector form, you can calculate the distance between any two data items. The next few sections will describe several different methods to calculate the distance between two vectors.

0.5.2 Distance

The Euclidean distance measurement, developed from the Pythagorean theorem, is based on the actual two-dimensional distance between two vectors. In other words, if you drew the vectors and measured them with a ruler, the difference between the two points would be the Euclidean distance measurement. Specifically, if you had two points **(x1,y1)** and **(x2,y2)**, the distance between the two would be described in the following way:

$$d = \sqrt{(x_2 - x_1)^2 + (y_2 - y_1)^2} \tag{1}$$

Figure 2 shows a two-dimensional Euclidean distance between two points.

Figure 2: Two-Dimensional Euclidean Distance

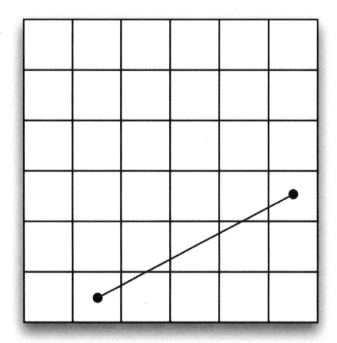

This formula is adequate to compare two vectors of length 2. However, most vectors are longer than two numbers. To calculate the Euclidean distance for vectors of any size, use the general form of the Euclidean distance equation.

Machine learning often utilizes the Euclidean distance measurement because it is a quick way to compare two vectors of numbers that have the same amount of elements. Consider three vectors, named vector **a**, vector **b**, and

0.5 Background Information

vector **c**. The Euclidean distance between array **a** and array **b** is 10. The Euclidean distance between array **a** and array **c** is 20. In this case, the contents of array **a** more closely match array **b** than they do array **c**.

Equation 2 shows a formula provided by Deza (2009) for calculating the Euclidean distance.

$$\mathrm{d}(\mathbf{p},\mathbf{q}) = \mathrm{d}(\mathbf{q},\mathbf{p}) = \sqrt{\sum_{i=1}^{n}(q_i - p_i)^2} \qquad (2)$$

The above equation shows us the Euclidean distance **d** between two arrays **p** and **q**. It also states that **d(p,q)** is the same as **d(q,p)**. In other words, the distance is the same no matter which end is the starting point. Calculating the Euclidean distance requires nothing more than summing the squares of the difference of each array element. After you calculate the sum of the squares, find the square root of this sum. This value is the Euclidean distance.

The following shows Equation 2 in pseudocode form:

```
sub euclidean(position1, position2):
  sum = 0
  for i from 0 to len(position1)-1:
    d = position1[i] - position2[i]
    sum = sum + d * d;

  return sqrt(sum);
```

0.5.3 Modeling with an RBF Network

Artificial intelligence uses models to accept an input vector and produce the correct output, allowing the model to recognize the input. For example, you might provide input for the four measurements in Fisher's iris data set and expect an output that tells you the species of the iris. In this section, we will introduce a radial-basis function (RBF) network (Bishop, 1996). The RBF network is a model for regression and classification. A regression model returns a number whereas a classification model returns a non-numeric value, such as an iris species.

In order to allow the input to generate the correct output, the RBF network uses a parameter vector, a model that specifies weights and coefficients. By adjusting a random parameter vector, the RBF network produces output consistent with the iris data set. The process of adjusting the parameter vector to produce the desired output is called training. Many different methods exist for training an RBF network. The parameter vectors also represent its long-term memory.

The next section will briefly review RBFs and describe the exact makeup of these vectors.

0.5.4 Radial-Basis Functions

Because many AI algorithms utilize radial-basis functions, they are a very important concept to understand. A radial-basis function is symmetric with respect to its center, which is usually somewhere along the x-axis. The RBF will reach its maximum value or peak at the center. Whereas a typical setting for the peak in RBF networks is 1, the center varies accordingly.

RBFs can have many dimensions. Regardless of the number of dimensions in the vector passed to the RBF, its output will always be a single scalar value.

RBFs are quite common in AI. We will start with the most prevalent, the Gaussian function. Figure 3 shows a graph of a 1D Gaussian function centered at 0.

0.5 Background Information

Figure 3: Gaussian Function

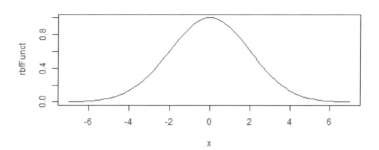

You might recognize the above curve as a normal distribution or a bell curve, which is a radial-basis function. These are commonly used to selectively scale numeric values, and a Gaussian function follows this model. Consider Figure 3. If you used this function to scale numeric values, the result would have maximum intensity at the center. As you moved from the center, the intensity would diminish in either the positive or negative directions.

Before we can look at the equation for the Gaussian RBF, we must consider how to process the multiple dimensions. RBFs accept multidimensional input. Using this input, an RBF returns a single value by calculating the distance between the input and the center vector of the RBF. This distance is called **r**. The RBF center and input to the RBF must always have the same number of dimensions for the calculation to occur. Once we calculate **r**, we can calculate the individual RBF function. All of the RBF functions use this calculated **r**.

Equation 3 shows how to calculate **r**.

$$r = ||\mathbf{x} - \mathbf{x}_i|| \qquad (3)$$

The double vertical bars that you see in the above equation signify that the function describes a distance. In certain cases, these distances can vary; however, RBFs typically utilize Euclidean distance. As a result, the examples that I provide in this book always apply the Euclidean distance. Therefore, **r** is simply the Euclidean distance between the center and the **x** vector. In each of the RBF functions in this section, I will use this value **r**. The equation for a Gaussian RBF is shown in Equation 4.

$$\phi(r) = e^{-r^2} \tag{4}$$

Once you've calculated **r**, calculating the RBF is fairly easy. The Greek letter PHI, which you see at the left of the equation, always represents the RBF. The constant e in Equation 4 represents Euler's number, or the natural base, and is approximately 2.71828.

0.5.5 Radial-Basis Function Networks

RBF networks provide a weighted summation of one or more radial-basis functions; each of these functions receives the weighted input attributes in order to predict the output. Consider the RBF network as a long equation that contains the parameter vector. Equation 5 shows the equation needed to calculate the output of this network.

$$f(X) = \sum_{i=1}^{N} a_i p(||b_i X - c_i||) \tag{5}$$

Note that the double vertical bars in the above equation signify to take the distance. Such symbols do not specify what distance algorithm to use; the choice is yours. In the above equation, **X** is the input vector of attributes; **c** is the vector center of the RBF; **p** is the chosen RBF (Gaussian, for example); **a** is the vector coefficient (or weight) for each RBF; and **b** specifies the vector coefficient to weight the input attributes.

In our example, we will apply an RBF network to the iris data set. Figure 4 provides a graphic representation of this application.

Figure 4: The RBF Network for the Iris Data

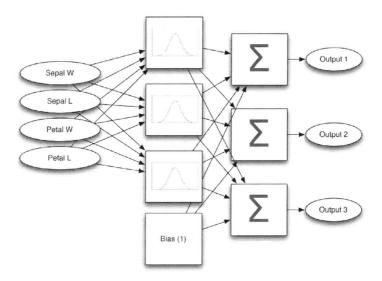

The above network contains four inputs (the length and width of petals and sepals) that indicate the features that describe each iris species. The above diagram assumes that we are using one-of-n encoding for the three different iris species. Using equilateral encoding for only two outputs is also possible. However, we will use one-of-n to keep things simple and arbitrarily choose three RBF functions. Even though additional RBF functions allow the model to learn more complex data sets, they require more time to process.

Arrows represent all coefficients from the equation. In Equation 5, **b** represents the arrows between the input attributes and the RBFs. Similarly, **a** represents the arrows between the RBFs and the summation. Notice also the bias box, which is a synthetic function that always returns a value of 1. Because the bias function's output is constant, the program does not require inputs. The weights from the bias to the summation specify the y-intercept for the equation. In short, bias is not always bad. This case demonstrates that bias is an important component to the RBF network. Bias nodes are also very common in neural networks.

Because multiple summations exist, you can see the development of a classification problem. The highest summation specifies the predicted class. A regression problem indicates that the model will output a single numeric value.

You will also notice that Figure 4 contains a bias node in the place where an additional RBF function might be used. However, the bias node does not accept any input–unlike the RBF. It always outputs a constant value of 1. Of course, this constant value of 1 is multiplied by a coefficient value, which always causes the coefficient to be directly added to the output, regardless of the input. When the input is 0, bias nodes are very useful because they allow the RBF layer to output values despite the low value of the input.

The long-term memory vector for the RBF network has several different components:

- Input coefficients
- Output/Summation coefficients
- RBF width scalars (same width in all dimensions)
- RBF center vectors

The RBF network will store all of these components as a single vector that will become its long-term memory. Then we will use an optimization algorithm to set the vector to values that will produce the correct iris species for the features presented. This book features several optimization algorithms that can train an RBF network.

In conclusion, this introduction provided a basic overview of vectors, distance, and RBF networks. Since this discussion included only the prerequisite material to understand Volume 2, refer to Volume 1 for a more thorough explanation of these topics.

Chapter 1

Population, Scoring, and Selection

- Populations
- Elitism
- Scoring
- Selection
- Scalability of Selection Algorithms

Artificial intelligence (AI) programming typically seeks solutions to problems. AI programming is not so different from traditional computer programming in its pursuit of solutions. However, the solution discovery process in AI is much more abstract and automated than traditional programming. AI solutions are often expressed as support vector machines (SVM), neural networks, random forests, genetic programs, hidden Markov models, and many more. Collectively, these AI techniques are referred to as models. A model takes input and produces an appropriate response. Our own human brain is the ultimate model.

You will often deal with many different models together as a population. Populations of models are used in many algorithms in order to solve a problem. We see the value of populations in the animal kingdom as certain species work together for survival. Birds flock to find food. Wolves usually hunt in packs. In this sense, a population can be considered as a group. Populations can also exist over time, evolving to adapt to their environment. For example, a small population of solutions may work to find the shortest route through a number of cities. Yet not every use of populations is so gradual; smaller units of a population can organize themselves to solve a problem. For example, a program might evolve an equation through many generations to better explain data.

Populations are necessary, but you must have a way to score their members. For example, in human society, we evaluate each other all the time for college admissions, promotions, and work projects. In AI, scoring allows a program to compare two competing solutions in a population in order to choose the best one. Additionally, scoring plays a role in many forms of selection that leads to the final solution.

Selection is the process by which a member of a population is chosen for a specific task. In nature, the selection process occurs when organisms that are well adapted to their environment survive to reproduce and continue the species. This is natural selection. AI uses both positive and negative forms of selection. Solutions with good scores are selected to help find better solutions. Conversely, solutions with bad scores are selected for termination in order to make way for better solutions.

This chapter will discuss population, scoring, and selection. You will be shown several techniques for each topic. These concepts lay the foundation for Chapter 2, where we will use selected solutions to find better solutions.

1.1 Understanding Populations

The use of the term "population" in this chapter is mostly compatible with the definitions seen in the Merriam-Webster Dictionary (2014). One such definition is "a group of people or animals of a particular kind that live in a place." For this book, populations are groups of potential solutions to a problem. These potential solutions are the same kind because these solutions are all intended to solve an identical problem. Sometimes members of the solution population will be broken into different species. However, I will still refer to members of these species as belonging to the same population.

Population is also a term commonly used in the study of statistics. A statistical population is defined as "a group of individual persons, objects, or items from which samples are taken for statistical measurement" (Merriam-Webster, 2014). In statistics, you frequently segment a population into smaller manageable groups called samples. Often we will sample from the population with bias towards a better score. Other times we may conduct a purely random sampling that gives each member of the population an equal opportunity to be chosen.

The population of solutions is also treated as a statistical population. As statisticians typically take samples of a population, an evolutionary algorithm will sample the population of solutions. Sampling typically involves taking a randomly selected group of one or more individuals from the population of potential solutions. These samples are then used for selection. Sampling for selection will be discussed later in this chapter.

1.1.1 Initial Population

A population size will not typically change as the evolutionary algorithm progresses. The population size is a hard limit. For example, if you specify a population size of 500, then there will always be 500 individuals. If 5 new individuals are born, then 5 must die to maintain the exact balance of 500 individuals. An initial population will be created with a count equal to this population size. The initial potential solutions that make up the initial population will be randomly generated. These initial random solutions will likely not be very good. However, some of these random solutions will score better than others.

The type of algorithm used in the program influences the population size. The members of a population can either be competitive or cooperative. Cooperative algorithms will typically start at a fixed size, and new members will never be added or deleted. Competitive populations will always create subsequent generations that are exactly made up of this fixed size. These generations are also called iterations. The next generation will be created from children generated from only the most suitable parents. Once the next generation of a competitive population hits this maximum number of offspring, no more children are born.

Animal behavior in nature is typically both competitive and cooperative. For example, a pack of wolves will cooperate and hunt together. Multiple wolf packs compete with each other for scarce resources. Additionally, competition within a pack will exist for selection of the alpha male. Nature-inspired algorithms are either competitive or cooperative; they are never implemented to be both. In this book, we will see examples of each type of algorithm, beginning with competitive populations.

1.1.2 Competition Among Population Members

Examples of competitive populations include genetic programming and genetic algorithms. Both of these algorithms create populations of potential solutions. Solutions that have better scores are more likely to be selected to mate and provide the next generation of the population. Other than mating, no direct cooperation occurs among the members of a competitive population.

A competitive population will always contain one or more solutions that have the top score. In the case of a tie, there will be multiple solutions with the top score. Another possible outcome is that the next generation may not contain a new solution that exceeds the best score of the previous generation. If this happens, the score for the best solution will drop, causing the training to take a step backwards. This outcome is usually undesirable.

You can resolve this problem with elitism, a training setting that specifies how many of the top scoring solutions are carried to the next generation. The algorithm is guaranteed not to revert to a worse score because the elitism setting always retains the best solution. However, it can be set to higher values than a single solution. Such values simply specify a larger number of the top-scoring solutions to advance to the next generation. Elitism is not the only way to prevent the population's top score from regressing to a lower score between generations. This regression can occur when none of the children scores as highly as the parents did. Tournaments can also prevent score regression. Tournament selection will be covered later in this chapter.

1.1.3 Cooperation Among Population Members

Not all populations in AI are competitive; cooperative populations exist in AI as well. Examples of cooperative populations include ant colony optimization (ACO) and particle swarm optimization (PSO). In these two algorithms, the individual potential solutions learn from each other. Information is shared between the individuals as they seek a good solution to the assigned problem.

Cooperative populations always track the best solution that their members have ever found. Cooperative algorithms are not greedy; they will accept a lesser solution in their search for the best solution. Because of this characteristic, keeping track of the best solution found so far is important. This record keeping allows you to revert to the best solution, even if the population members have moved on to lesser solutions.

Like competitive algorithms, cooperative algorithms are also iterative. However, a single cooperative iteration does not replace the previous population with a new generation. Iteration for a cooperative algorithm simply represents one complete pass of each potential solution as it evaluates its effectiveness and receives a score. At the end of each iteration cycle, all potential solutions collaborate and adjust their solution parameters to maximize their scores.

1.1.4 Phenotype and Genotype

Phenotype and genotype, two terms that come directly from biology, are important to some nature-inspired algorithms. A genotype is the genetic information from which an organism grows. The phenotype is the actual organism that results from the genotype. Identical twins are a good example of the difference between phenotype and genotype. The same genotype is shared by the identical twins. However, the twins mature into different people with slightly varied physical characteristics. In AI, the same genotype grows into two marginally different phenotypes.

Nevertheless, most evolutionary algorithms do not differentiate between phenotype and genotype. There is no differentiation between a potential solution's genotype and the actual solution phenotype that is evaluated. Therefore, I will follow this guideline and not differentiate between phenotype and genotype in the evolutionary algorithms that I discuss.

One example of a nature-inspired algorithm that does differentiate genotype and phenotype is the HyperNEAT neural network (Stanley, 2009). HyperNEAT is not a topic covered in this book; however, it is a planned topic for Volume 3 of this series.

1.1.5 Populations on Islands

Geographic separation can have a great impact on the evolution of natural populations of organisms. Islands such as Tasmania, the Galapagos Islands, and Madagascar all have very different ecological characteristics than those of the closest mainland. Additionally, the interactions between populations on and off the island may change over time. Islands may have once been part of the mainland. Land bridges may come and go. These events govern the degree of separation between individual populations.

The concept of an island can also be used in nature-inspired algorithms to have multiple populations that are largely independent of each other, just as real islands separate populations. The algorithm may also choose to allow occasional interaction between the islands. This intermittent interaction is similar to a land bridge or other geological event that allowed organisms to travel between ecosystems.

The island concept is most commonly applied to competitive populations. Separating potential solutions into multiple populations allows new innovations to evolve without being threatened by established populations. Occasional interaction can be allowed among the islands, and it permits foreign solutions from other islands to introduce new ideas.

The multiple population concepts can also be applied to cooperative populations, which are analogous to a corporation creating multiple teams to tackle the same problem. These teams may occasionally collaborate on an idea, but they are largely autonomous. One could consider Xerox PARC as a separate island from the larger Xerox. Even though PARC likely collaborates with the greater Xerox from time to time, their separation allows them to create some very unique solutions to computing problems.

Ultimately, the concept of multiple populations has some very practical aspects. It is very compatible with distributed computing. One of the most difficult aspects of any distributed computing problem is synchronization between the individual computers that comprise the computing cluster. Because the separate populations are inherently autonomous of each other, the algorithm does not require synchronization, which makes the task easy to implement on a parallel system.

1.2 Scoring Populations

To be able to score members of a population is very valuable. The score of a population member determines the suitability of the potential solution represented by that population member. Most evolutionary algorithms can either minimize or maximize a score. You need to decide if a low score or high score is good. Some human games, such as golf, seek a minimized or low score. Other games like football seek a maximized or high score.

Members are scored as they are added to the population. The score for a potential solution is typically stored on the same object as the solution. This storage location prevents the program from continually needing to recalculate the score. Initially, you need to score each member of the random population. If a population member changes, then its score also needs to be recalculated. If a new population member is added, then its score needs to be determined.

The exact means by which an individual is scored depends on the type of problem being solved. A fitness function evaluates the potential solution and assigns a score. For example, a simple fitness function may compare expected outputs from a model to the actual outputs obtained from the models. Additionally, you can create more complex fitness functions that use customized program code to evaluate a potential solution. The only requirement of a fitness function is that it must provide a numeric score to evaluate a potential solution in comparison with other potential solutions. Fitness functions are sometimes referred to as loss functions or objective functions.

Scoring is typically the performance bottleneck for an evolutionary algorithm. Often you will need to run a lengthy data set through each new potential solution added to the population. The score from this type of data set is typically the average difference between the actual and expected outputs of each element in the training set.

1.3 Selecting from Populations

Selection is the process by which you select one or more potential solutions from the population. This selection process is often called sampling. You can

1.4 Truncation Selection

choose from a variety of different selection processes. Each approach has its own strengths and weaknesses. The most common selection algorithms include the following:

- Truncation Selection
- Tournament Selection
- Fitness-Proportionate Selection
- Stochastic Universal Sampling

These selection algorithms will be discussed in the next sections.

1.4 Truncation Selection

Truncation selection is one of the most basic selection algorithms. In his paper on the Breeder Genetic Algorithm, Heinz Muhlenbein (1993) stated that truncation selection requires that the population be sorted according to fitness. Once sorted, some proportion (e.g., 1/3) is chosen to become the breeding population. Potential solutions are then sampled from the breeding population to help produce the next generation. The exact means by which the next generation is created is discussed in Chapter 2, "Crossover and Mutation." Figure 1.1 shows how the total population is divided by the truncation selection.

Figure 1.1: Truncation Selection

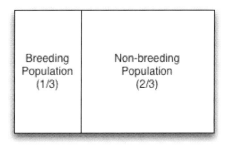

The truncation selection algorithm can be represented by the following pseudocode shown in Listing 1.1:

Listing 1.1: Truncation Selection Pseudocode

```
sub truncate_select(breeding_ratio, sorted_population)
  # Sort the population. For efficiency you should move
  # this outside the selection function and perform the sort
  # once for each batch of selections you will perform.
  sort(sorted_population)
  # Determine the size of the breeding population.
  count = len(sorted_population) * breeding_ratio
  # Obtain a uniformly distributed (all numbers have
  # equal probability) single random number
  # between 0 and count.
  index = uniform_random(0, count)
  # Return the selected element.
  return sorted_population[index]
```

One of the biggest limitations to the truncation selection algorithm is that the population must be sorted. This sorting severely limits the ability of the algorithm to be parallelized for multicore and distributed computing. You must constantly keep the entire population in a known sorted state. As a result, this algorithm does not scale well for a large population where you might have many different selections running in parallel.

Additionally, because parents only produce children and do not join the next generation, the possibility exists that none of the children meets or exceeds the score of the best solution in the previous generation. Consequently, you should use elitism to select one or more of the top solutions to be copied directly to the next generation. Without elitism, your best score may decrease between iterations.

1.5 Tournament Selection

Tournament selection is another popular selection algorithm for evolutionary algorithms. Easy to implement, it solves the scalability issues of truncation selection. Tournament selection works by looping through a series of rounds, always allowing the winner to advance to the next round. The number of rounds is a training setting. For each round, you must choose two random individuals in the population. The better scoring individual goes onto the next round (Miller, 1995).

Tournament selection can be used to select either fit or unfit individuals from the population. You simply run an inverse tournament where a less fit score wins. An example of tournament selection is shown in Figure 1.2.

Figure 1.2: Tournament Selection

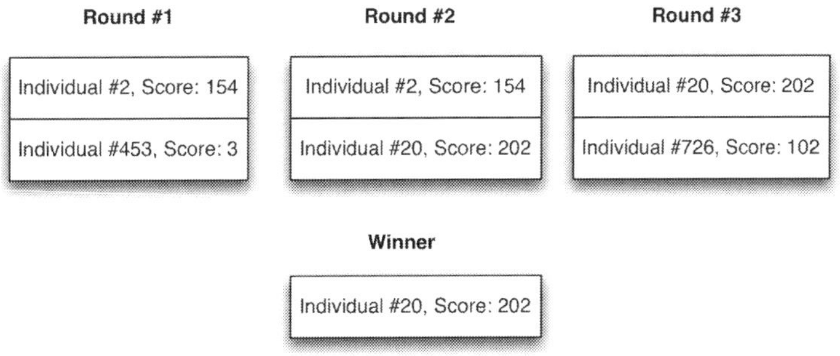

Round #1	Round #2	Round #3
Individual #2, Score: 154	Individual #2, Score: 154	Individual #20, Score: 202
Individual #453, Score: 3	Individual #20, Score: 202	Individual #726, Score: 102

Winner

Individual #20, Score: 202

For Figure 1.2, we used three rounds. For round one, we chose two members at random. Individual #2 had the best score and went on to round two. For round two, a new contender was chosen. Individual #20, with its score of 202 won round two and advanced to round three. For round three, Individual #20 retained its champion status and won the entire tournament. This algorithm is summarized in Listing 1.2.

Listing 1.2: Tournament Selection

```
# Perform a tournament selection with the specified number of
# rounds. A high score is considered desirable (maximize)
sub tournament_select(rounds, population)
  # Nothing has been selected yet
  champ = null
  # Perform the rounds. There is a "round zero" where the first
  # contender is chosen becomes the champ by default.
  for x from 0 to rounds:
    # Choose a random contender from the population.
    contender = uniform_random(population)

    # If we do not yet have a champ,
    # then the current contender is the champ by default.
    if champ is null:
      champ = contender
    # If the contender has a better score, it is the new champ.
    else if contender.score > champ.score:
      champ = contender

  return champ
```

As you can see from the above code, no sorting was required. You can also create an inverse selection by flipping to a "less than" operator to a "greater than" operator.

Tournament selection also allows you to break the typical generational model that evolutionary operators often use. Breaking the generational model offers great efficiencies for parallel processing. The lack of a generational model is also closer to biology. Since babies are born every day, we don't have a clearly defined moment for the beginning and ending of one human generation.

1.5 Tournament Selection

To abandon the generational model, use tournament selection and choose two fit parents that will produce a child. To choose an unfit population member, run a reverse tournament. The unfit population member is killed and replaced by the new child. This truncation model eliminates the need for elitism. The best solution will never be replaced because a reverse tournament will never select it.

This algorithm is very efficient for parallel processing. The parallel processing loop might look something like Listing 1.3.

Listing 1.3: Parallel Evolutionary Algorithm

```
best = null
required_score = [the score you want]
# Loop so long as we either do not yet have a best,
# or the best.score is less than required_score.
parallel while best is null or best.score < required_score:
  # Lock, and choose two parents.  We do not want changes
  # to the population while picking the parents.
  lock:
    parent1 = tournament_select(5,population)
    parent2 = null

    # Pick a second parent.
    # Do not select the same individual for both parents.
    while parent2 == null or parent1 == parent2:
      parent2 = uniform_random(population)
  # Parents are chosen, so we can exit the lock
  # and use crossover to create a child.
  child = crossover(parent1,parent2)
  child.score = score(child)
  # we must now choose (and kill) a victim.
  # The victim is replaced by the new child.
  lock:
    victim = reverse_select(5,population)
    population.remove(victim)
    population.add(child)
  # See if the child is the new best.
    if child.score>best.score
      best = child
```

The above code includes two locked sections. A single thread will only execute one locked section at a time. Other threads must wait when a thread is inside the locked area. For efficiency purposes, the code inside a locked section should be optimized to execute very quickly. The first lock simply chooses two parents. The time-consuming part will be scoring the child. The child is created and scored outside of any locks. This method is good because nothing needs to wait on the scoring. It is always good practice to keep time-consuming code outside of the locks. The final lock chooses a victim and inserts the child. We also track the best solution found so far.

You might have noticed the **crossover** function above. Crossover is one of several methods for adding new members to the population. Crossover will be discussed in Chapter 2.

Tournament selection is also biologically plausible. To survive to the next day, an individual does not need to be able to outrun the fastest predator in the population. The individual only needs to outrun the predators that it encounters on any given day.

1.6 How to Choose Round Count

The number of rounds is a training setting, just like population count. Even though training settings are not part of the final solution, they will affect how quickly you find an adequate solution. Typically, training settings are set through trial and error. I usually start with a population size of 1,000 and a round count equal to 5.

Because I wanted to see how round count affected the score of the individual selected, I ran a small experiment on them to determine their influence. I created a population of 1,000 individuals; each individual had a score between 0 and 999, depending on its position in the list. I then performed tournament selection 100,000 times on the population and returned the average score selected. The goal was to have the tournament selection return fit individuals. As you can see, as the number of rounds increased, so did the average score.

```
Rounds: 1, Avg Score: 665
Rounds: 2, Avg Score: 749
Rounds: 3, Avg Score: 799
Rounds: 4, Avg Score: 832
Rounds: 5, Avg Score: 857
```

1.7 Fitness-Proportionate Selection

```
Rounds: 6, Avg Score: 874
Rounds: 7, Avg Score: 888
Rounds: 8, Avg Score: 899
Rounds: 9, Avg Score: 908
Rounds: 10, Avg Score: 915
```

Obviously, we want fit individuals to be selected. I found a round count of 5 to be a good tradeoff since it was close to the 90th percentile and not an excessive number of rounds. Nevertheless, even though the rounds are computationally cheap, we do not always want to choose parents in the top 1%. We do want to encourage some variety.

1.7 Fitness-Proportionate Selection

Fitness-proportionate selection, also known as roulette wheel selection, is a popular selection method for evolutionary algorithms (Back, 1995). This technique resembles a roulette wheel as individuals occupy a section of the roulette wheel that is proportional to the desirability of their score. When one spins the roulette wheel, more desirable individuals have a greater likelihood of selection. Figure 1.3 shows how you might visualize this type of roulette wheel.

Figure 1.3: Fitness-Proportionate Selection

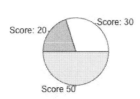

The above diagram shows how scores of 20, 30 and 50 are distributed around the wheel. A score of 50 has a 50% chance of being selected. The scores do not necessarily need to align to even percentage numbers. The proportions will simply adjust to the sum of the scores. Fitness proportionate-selection could allow the least fit individual to be chosen. Yet tournament or truncation selection would never choose the least fit individual. This selection process is not necessarily bad. Diversity in the selection process sometimes creates interesting results since it allows new ideas to enter the population.

Several different implementations of the fitness-proportionate algorithms exist. All such selection algorithms will either require access to the entire population, or they need to sort the population. This algorithm makes fitness-proportionate selection undesirable from a parallelization standpoint. Sorting or summing the entire population is difficult when running in parallel.

Listing 1.4 shows a pseudocode implementation of fitness-proportionate selection.

Listing 1.4: Fitness-Proportionate Selection

```
# Select an individual using fitness-proportionate selection
sub fitness_proportion_select(population)
  # Calculate the total score, so that proportions
  # can be determined.
  total_score = 0
  for individual in population:
    total_score = total_score + individual.score

  r = random_uniform(0,1)

  # Spin through the areas on the wheel until we pass point "r".
  covered_so_far = 0
  for individual in population:
    covered_so_far = covered_so_far +
      (individual.score/total_score)
    # Have we covered the random point (r) yet?
    if r<covered_so_far:
      return individual

  # Should not ever happen.
  return null
```

The above algorithm first calculates the sum of all of the scores. This process allows us to calculate the percentage of the wheel that each individual score covers. The calculation required is a simple percent calculation. We then generate a random number in the range between 0 and 1. We now start at 0 and begin adding the size of each population member to the sum. Once the sum exceeds the previously generated random number, we have found the part of the wheel that contains our random number. Larger areas of the wheel have a higher probability of being selected. Fitness-proportionate selection can have bad performance when a member of the population has a really large score in comparison with other members. This type of individual will dominate selection.

1.8 Stochastic Universal Sampling

Whereas fitness-proportionate selection utilizes repeated random selection to choose several individuals from the population, James Baker (1987) introduced stochastic universal sampling (SUS) to use a single random value to sample the number of requested individuals. These individuals are selected at evenly spaced intervals. This type of selection gives weaker (according to their fitness) members of the population a chance to be chosen and thus reduces the unfair nature of fitness-proportionate selection.

Figure 1.4 graphically shows how stochastic universal sampling works.

Figure 1.4: Stochastic Universal Sampling

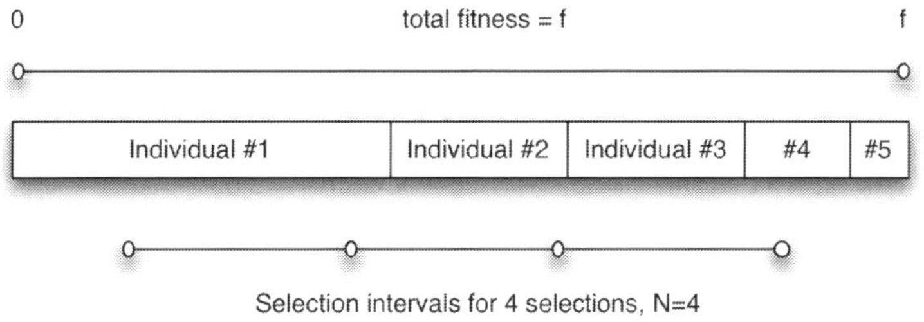

One very important difference between stochastic universal sampling and the selection methods previously seen is that SUS works best when you select all of the needed individuals at the same time. The previous selection methods choose individuals separately. The above figure illustrates the selection of 4 individuals from the population. You will notice that individual #1 is selected twice, then individual #2 and finally individual #4. We are requesting 4 individuals from a population size of 5, so receiving a single individual multiple times is a possible outcome.

The line at the bottom of Figure 1.4 shows the individuals being selected at regular intervals. The leftmost position of the line is the only random number generated. It is generated between 0 and the length of each line segment. The line segments are all equal to f/N (total fitness divided by number of individuals requested). Once this initial random point is selected, each additional individual is selected by moving forward.

Listing 1.5 shows the pseudocode needed to implement stochastic universal sampling.

Listing 1.5: Stochastic Universal Sampling (SUS)

```
# N is the number of individuals to select.
sub stochastic_universal_sampling(population, N)
  # Calculate the total score of the population.
  f = 0

  # Add up individual scores.
  for individual in population:
    f = f + individual.score

  # Calculate the distance between the pointers.
  p = f/N

  # Choose random number between 0 and p
  start = random_uniform(0,p)

  # Define points
  points = []
  for i from 0 to (N-1):
    points[i] = start + (i*p)

  # Perform basic roulette wheel select
  selected = []
  i = 0
```

1.8 Stochastic Universal Sampling

```
# Loop over points
for p in points:
  while population[i].score < p:
    i = i + 1
    selected.add(population[i])

# Return selected individuals
return selected
```

As you can see, SUS starts by calculating the total score of the population. SUS also requires that the population be sorted, as in Figure 1.4, due to the high probability that the algorithm will choose the most prevalent individuals regardless of the order (Baker, 1987). Although SUS is useful in situations where a few highly scored individuals are dominating fitness-proportionate selection, this algorithm does not work as well with large data and highly parallelized situations. Tournament selection is a good alternative when a single high-scoring individual is dominating selection. Tournament selection will not be dominated because each individual has an equal chance of entering the tournament. SUS might pick extremely weak individuals, but they will always be eliminated in tournaments. This outcome may or may not be desirable.

1.8.1 Choosing a Selection Algorithm

With several selection algorithms available, you might wonder which one to choose. I almost always use tournament selection because it is extremely fast and scalable. The main downside to tournament selection is that very weak individuals will often be eliminated before they have a chance to refine and adapt through a few generations. This outcome can cause stagnation in the best scores obtained by the population.

If your population is stagnating, you might want to try stochastic universal sampling. This choice will allow weaker members to be chosen some of the time. If performance becomes an issue, you can disable the sort. You still have to track total fitness of the population. However, total fitness can be calculated once and then adjusted as members of the population are born and die. These tweaks can make stochastic universal sampling quite scalable and parallelizable.

1.9 Chapter Summary

This chapter introduced populations and selections. A population is a group of potential solutions to a problem. Populations can be either cooperative or competitive, depending on the evolutionary algorithm that is in use. The population progresses through iterations and slowly refines its solution to a problem.

A cooperative population is a group of a certain number of individuals that work together on a problem. Ant colony optimization (ACO) and particle swarm optimization (PSO) are two examples of cooperative algorithms. In both of these cases, the individuals work together and share information to find better solutions to the problem being studied.

A competitive population pits members against each other. Survival of the fittest plays out, and only the best individuals become parents. This behavior allows them to impart their traits to the next generation. In the end, the individual with the best score becomes the final solution to the problem.

Scoring is the process where numeric scores are assigned to individuals in the population. The objective might be a low or high score. Some algorithms require the population to be sorted according to the score. Such algorithms do not scale well and are difficult to adapt for parallel processing and distributed computing.

Selection is the process by which individuals are chosen from the population to help create the next generation. Truncation selection is a simple algorithm that randomly selects an individual from a definable top percentage of the population. Tournament selection takes the top individual from a group randomly selected from the population. Fitness-proportionate selection, or roulette wheel selection, randomly chooses an individual based on its score. Stochastic universal sampling selects individuals at regular intervals. Tournament selection is the best general-purpose selection algorithm.

In conclusion, this chapter focused on how to select individuals so they can bestow their attributes to the next generation. In Chapter 2, I will introduce crossover and mutation in order to describe how the chosen individuals actually affect and produce the next generation.

1.9 Chapter Summary

Chapter 2

Crossover and Mutation

- Evolutionary Algorithms
- Splice Crossover
- Repeating Genes
- Shuffle Mutation
- Perturb Mutation

Chapter 1 introduced populations and showed the selection process of suitable parents. Once the selection process chooses the most favorable parents, specific algorithms are required in order to cause those parents to produce the next generation. These evolutionary algorithms are essential components in competitive populations. In fact, they represent the only way that the population adds new individuals. This book deals with three different types:

- Elitism
- Mutation
- Crossover

Broadening the first chapter's treatment of these topics, Chapter 2 will demonstrate how an evolutionary algorithm employs elitism, mutation, and crossover to create successive generations of solutions. Ideally, each subsequent generation will improve upon the previous generation.

2.1 Evolutionary Algorithms

Many different evolutionary algorithms exist, and the majority of them utilize evolutionary operators such as fitness functions, selection, elitism, crossover, and mutation. Depending on the evolutionary algorithm that you choose, the implementation of these evolutionary operators varies. Later chapters will explain in more detail the following evolutionary algorithms:

- Genetic Algorithms (GA)
- Genetic Programming (GP)
- Human-Based Genetic Algorithm (HBGA)
- Ant Colony Optimization (ACO)
- Particle Swarm Optimization (PSO)

Figure 2.1: Evolutionary Algorithms

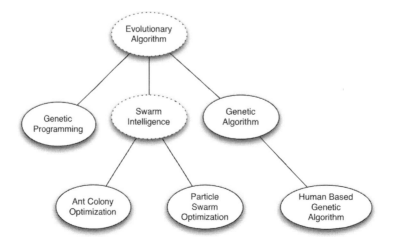

2.1 Evolutionary Algorithms

The above diagram illustrates the connections among the evolutionary algorithms presented in this book. Dotted lines enclose the ovals of evolutionary algorithm and swarm intelligence to indicate that they represent abstract types of algorithms, not actual ones.

The algorithms in Figure 2.1 have many commonalities. Every algorithm in the diagram is population based, and they all deal with populations of potential solutions that must be scored. In other words, you will always use some type of scoring function with an evolutionary algorithm.

Some of the algorithms use competitive populations. Genetic programming, genetic algorithms, and human-based genetic algorithms use competitive populations. As a result, they will utilize the elitism, mutation, and crossover. The configuration settings determine the degree to which you use these algorithms. Additionally, the population size is usually fixed. In short, competitive evolutionary algorithms use four configuration settings that are listed below with their common default values:

- Population Size: 1,000

- Elitism Count: 3

- Crossover Percent: 0.8

- Mutation Percent: 0.2

The above settings are a good starting point for evolutionary algorithms. The elitism value of 3 indicates that we will always copy the top three individuals to the next generation. The crossover and mutation percent values define the ratio that is necessary to create the next generation. This ratio means that 80% of the individuals chosen to move to the next generation will be a combination of parameters from two selected parents, and 20% will be copies of only one parent with a small number of random parameter changes. Of course, the crossover and mutation percent values must sum to 1.0.

2.2 Solution Encoding

Thus far, we have examined populations of potential solutions. Now, we need to explain what a solution actually resembles. Most evolutionary algorithms require that the potential solutions be fixed-length arrays. Each solution must have the same array length as the other solutions. Genetic algorithms follow this guideline even though it may seem limiting. One of the most challenging aspects of using an evolutionary algorithm is representing solutions as fixed-length arrays. Therefore, Chapter 3, "Genetic Algorithms," will include examples of representing several solutions as fixed-length arrays.

Determining the nature of the data in your fixed-length array is essential. If your array is numerical, or continuous, then each array element represents a floating-point number. Values such as percentages, order quantities or salaries are examples of numeric values. If you are dealing with integer values such as order quantities, you will need to make sure that your mutation and crossover functions respect the integer nature of your numbers.

If your values are categorical, then they are discrete values, such as employees, cities, building components, or ingredients. Values that are not numerical will affect the way that you mutate this type of array. The next section includes an analysis of these arrays.

In an evolutionary algorithm, using structures of variable length as your solutions is possible. However, you'll have to design your own crossover and mutation operators if you use variable-length structures. We will see an example of variable-length structures in Chapter 4, "Genetic Programming." As we will evolve equations using genetic programming, the length of the equations will certainly vary.

2.3　Mutation

Mutation in evolutionary algorithms differs considerably from the biological concept of mutation. A biological mutation is a change in an organism's DNA sequence that can be beneficial or harmful. It is typically caused by radiation or a chemical reaction. Mutation in evolutionary algorithms is asexual reproduction. In other words, mutation is a way to create a child based on the traits of only one parent.

Mutation allows the potential solution to produce a slightly refined child in the next generation. Because the possibility exists that the potential solution is already optimal, it receives only a few refinements from the parent. These changes to the child are mutation. They are usually random. This is different from nature, where an existing organism experiences the mutation. For evolutionary organisms, mutation is simply a form of reproduction.

Individuals in evolutionary algorithms that reproduce both sexually (crossover) and asexually (mutation) are very common. Many organisms in nature also reproduce both sexually and asexually, including aphids, slime molds, sea anemones, and many plants. When the animal or plant has just one parent, mutation represents the only way that the offspring can vary from the parents.

Mutation and crossover are both essential parts of evolutionary algorithms. Crossover recombines the traits of the best solutions; however, crossover cannot introduce new traits. Mutation is the process in which completely new traits are introduced into the potential solutions. Used together, crossover and mutation allow new traits to be discovered and subsequently crafted into new solutions.

In the next few sections, we will examine the ways that nature-inspired algorithms implement mutation. As previously discussed, when choosing a mutation algorithm, you must consider if your solution array is numerical or categorical. However, if your solution array is both numerical and categorical, you will likely need to create your own mutation operator that is a hybrid of the algorithms presented in the next sections. The first hybrid we will study is shuffle mutation.

2.3.1 Shuffle Mutation

Shuffle mutation can be used with both categorical and numeric solution arrays. Although shuffle mutation is flexible enough to be used for either solution array type, it is rarely used with numeric solution arrays (Mitchell, 1998) because shuffle mutation is simply changing the order of the solution array. Shuffle mutation does not change the actual values in the array. To understand this idea, consider if we had a parent solution array that held the values 1 through 5.

```
Parent: [1, 2, 3, 4, 5]
```

A shuffle mutation usually works by performing one or more random flips of two array components. After a shuffle mutation, the above parent might produce the following offspring:

```
Offspring: [1, 5, 3, 4, 2]
```

As you can see from the above offspring, we flipped the second and fifth positions. If you have very large solution arrays, you might want to flip positions more than one time. However, you do not want to flip them too many times because the offspring must bear some resemblance to the parent. Otherwise, you are randomly searching for better solutions. Another important consideration is that the mutation operation does not change the parent. In fact, the only purpose of mutation is creating a descendant.

Listing 2.1 shows the pseudocode for shuffle mutation.

Listing 2.1: Shuffle Mutation

```
# Shuffle mutate the specified parent "flips" number of times.
sub shuffle_mutate(parent, flips)
  # Create the offspring
  offspring = clone(parent)
  # Perform the requested number of flips
  for i from 1 to flips:
    # Perform the flip, convert random num to an int
    index1 = int(random_uniform(0, len(parent)-1))
    index2 = -1
    # Choose a second index that is different than the first.
    # We do not want to swap the same index.
    while index2==-1 or index1==index2:
```

2.3 Mutation

```
        index2 = int(random_uniform(0,len(parent)-1))
    # Perform the swap.
    temp = offspring[index1]
    offspring[index1] = offspring[index2]
    offspring[index2] = temp
    return offspring
```

As you can see from this code, we simply choose two elements and flip them. However, we have to ensure that the two indexes are not identical. If we did not perform this check, the children would often be exact clones of the parent. Because cloning is not the purpose of mutation, swapping the same index should be avoided.

The above function does not guarantee that multiple flips will be unique. Using two flips could result in a clone. For example, the first flip might choose to flip indexes #3 and #5. If the second flip also chooses these same indexes, the second flip will undo the first. Thus, the child that results from these flips is identical to the parent. In terms of algorithm speed to find a high score, I have discovered that additional checking does not cause any significant gains. As a result, I typically use only a single flip. The problem of parent cloning is not worth the additional memory and complexity of tracking each flip.

2.3.2 Perturb Mutation

Perturb mutation works well with numeric solution arrays but is completely incompatible with categorical arrays. Perturb mutation is implemented by randomly increasing or decreasing each numeric value in the array. A configuration variable is provided for perturb mutation to specify the degree of randomness to apply to each array member (Mitchell, 1998).

Consider the following parent solution:

```
Parent: [1.0, 2.0, 3.0, 4.0, 5.0]
```

Running the above parent through a perturb mutation could produce the following offspring:

```
Offspring: [
  1.0421760973088268,
  1.8180609054044645,
  2.985473376997353,
  4.235569162430029,
  4.87239116615422]
```

As you can see in the previous figures, we added a random amount of noise to each number because the basic series from the parent is still evident. Each number increased or decreased by a relatively small random amount. Listing 2.2 shows the pseudocode that implements perturb mutation.

Listing 2.2: Perturb Mutation

```
sub perturb_mutate(parent, perturb_amount):
  # Copy the parent to the child.
  child = clone(parent)

  # Loop over and mutate each element in the child.
  for i from 0 to len(parent)-1:
    value = parent[i]
    # Mutate by an amount that is proportional to the value
    # in the parent.
    delta = value *
      random_uniform(-perturb_amount, perturb_amount)
    child[i] = child[i] + delta

  return child
```

The code in Listing 2.2 shows the process. First, copy the parent to the child. Then mutate each element in the child by an amount equal to the current value scaled by a random percent in the range from negative **perturb_amount** to positive **perturb_amount**. Make sure to consider the current value of the array so as not to apply a value that is disproportionally too large or small. For example, if we were to use a **perturb_amount** of 0.5, and the current value of the array element is 10, we would generate a random number in the range between -0.5 and 0.5. This random number would be multiplied by the current value 10, giving a value in the range -5 to 5. Adding this figure to the value of 10 means that the child could end up in the range 5 to 15.

Many different implementations exist for perturbing mutation. Some other variations include the following:

- Perturb using a range equal to the normal distribution with the standard deviation as a training setting.

- Provide a probability that each element is perturbed, rather than perturbing every element.

- Randomly select an array element and perturb just that element.

Generally, I use a perturbing system like the pseudocode provided in Listing 2.2. Scaling to the current value of the array value is very useful in later training when the changes to the array become smaller as we are ideally nearing an optimal solution.

2.4 Crossover

Crossover allows sexual reproduction in evolutionary algorithms. In nature, crossover occurs when a single male and female mate and produce offspring. Hermaphrodite organisms, such as snails, can play the role of either mother or father. Crossover in nature-inspired algorithms differs considerably from crossover in nature. Most evolutionary algorithms permit any individual to perform crossover with any other individual since the solutions that you are evolving do not have genders. In other words, mothers and fathers do not exist in crossover. Therefore, selecting a male and female individual for crossover is not necessary.

Even though most crossover implementations have two parents, this setup is not a strict requirement. I first saw an algorithm that used groups of more than two parents in the article, *Genetic Algorithms–Useful, Fun and Easy* by David Snell (2013).

In short, programmers can implement crossover in many ways. The next chapter will highlight some of these applications.

2.4.1 Splice Crossover

Both numeric and categorical data use splice crossover. It works by taking two parents and producing two children (Mitchell, 1998). The parents are split according to two cut points, and this split produces three sub-arrays for each parent that are subsequently spliced together to produce two children. Each child gets one sub-array from one parent and two sub-arrays from the other parent. You can see this split in Figure 2.2.

Figure 2.2: Splice Crossover

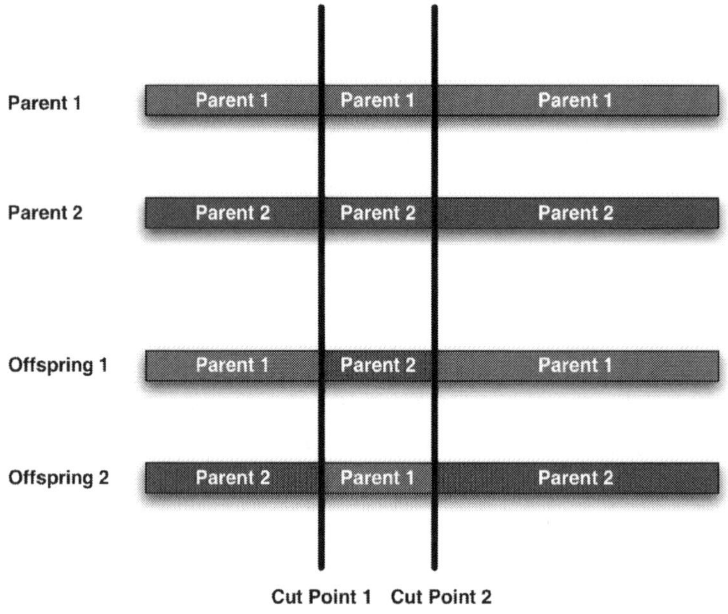

	Segment 1	Segment 2	Segment 3
Parent 1	Parent 1	Parent 1	Parent 1
Parent 2	Parent 2	Parent 2	Parent 2
Offspring 1	Parent 1	Parent 2	Parent 1
Offspring 2	Parent 2	Parent 1	Parent 2

Cut Point 1   Cut Point 2

The program selects two random cut points, as can be seen above. The program chooses the first cut point randomly. Adding the cut length to the first cut chooses the second cut point. The cut length is a training setting that defines the length of the middle cut section, and it remains constant during the evolutionary algorithm.

2.4 Crossover

Now, we will explain how an actual array is processed with splice crossover. Consider two parents, labeled parent 1 and parent 2:

```
Parent 1: [1, 2, 3, 4, 5, 6, 7, 8, 9, 10]
Parent 2: [10, 9, 8, 7, 6, 5, 4, 3, 2, 1]
```

Splice crossover could create two offspring from the parents listed above.

```
Offspring 1: [1, 2, 3, 7, 6, 5, 4, 3, 2, 10]
Offspring 2: [10, 9, 8, 4, 5, 6, 7, 8, 9, 1]
```

As you can see, both offspring contain elements from each of the parents. You may also have noticed that parents 1 and 2 have repeating numbers within their respective arrays. Because the two offspring took random splices from both parents, this process introduced repeats to the children. Furthermore, the complete set of numbers is no longer present in either child. This result might not be a problem if you are trying to optimize the order of a series of objects. Nevertheless, these repeats will likely cause issues in the solution.

In the next section, you will observe a demonstration of a non-repeating version of splice crossover. Listing 2.3 shows the pseudocode that implements the splice crossover operator that allows repeating.

Listing 2.3: Splice Crossover

```
sub slice_crossover(parent1, parent2, cut_length):
  # Allocate two child arrays. Same length.
  offspring1 = alloc(len(parent1))
  offspring2 = alloc(len(parent1))
  # The array must be cut at two positions, determine them.
  cutpoint1 = int(random_uniform(len(parent1) - cut_length))
  cutpoint2 = cutpoint1 + cut_length

  # Handle the middle section.
  for i from 0 to len(parent1)-1:
    if (i >= cutpoint1) and (i < cutpoint2):
      offspring1[i] = parent2[i]
      offspring2[i] = parent1[i]
  # Handle outer sections.
  for i from 0 to len(parent1)-1:
    if (i < cutpoint1) or (i >= cutpoint2):
      offspring1[i] = parent1[i]
```

```
        offspring2[i] = parent2[i]

# Return the two children as an array.
return [offspring1, offspring2]
```

The next section demonstrates a version of the splice crossover that does not allow repeating.

2.4.2 No Repeat Splice Crossover

Performing a crossover operation while not allowing any repeating entries in the child can be important. Nevertheless, this consideration does not apply to the shuffle mutate operator. Because the shuffle mutate operator is working with a single parent, the operator will not introduce any repeats that do not already exist.

The non-repeating version of the splice crossover operator works very similarly to the repeating version. The only difference is that the crossover operator keeps a list of elements that are already used.

To see the results of the non-repeating version of the splice operator, consider the following two parents:

```
Parent 1: [1, 2, 3, 4, 5, 6, 7, 8, 9, 10]
Parent 2: [10, 9, 8, 7, 6, 5, 4, 3, 2, 1]
```

This splicing results in the following two offspring when used with cut points after elements 1 and 7:

```
Offspring 1: [1, 9, 8, 7, 6, 5, 4, 2, 3, 10]
Offspring 2: [10, 2, 3, 4, 5, 6, 7, 9, 8, 1]
```

As you can see, the repeating elements are not in the offspring. Additionally, the offspring still have a complete set of the numbers from both parents. Listing 2.4 contains the pseudocode to create a non-repeating splice crossover operator.

2.4 Crossover

Listing 2.4: Splice Crossover (non-repeating version)

```
# Find unused elements in a list, and mark them used.
sub find_unused(source, used):
  for x in source:
    if not x in used:
      used[x] = 1
      return x
  # Should not happen, we ran out of elements.
  return -1
sub slice_crossover_nr(parent1, parent2, cut_length):
  # Allocate two child arrays. Same length.
  offspring1 = alloc(len(parent1))
  offspring2 = alloc(len(parent1))

  # Two maps to hold already used list
  used1 = {}
  used2 = {}

  # The array must be cut at two positions, determine them.
  cutpoint1 = int(random_uniform(len(parent1) - cut_length))
  cutpoint2 = cutpoint1 + cut_length;

  # Handle the middle section.
  for i from 0 to len(parent1)-1:
    if (i >= cutpoint1) and (i < cutpoint2):
      offspring1[i] = parent2[i]
      offspring2[i] = parent1[i]
      used[offspring1[i]] = 1
      used[offspring2[i]] = 1
  # Handle outer sections.
  for i from 0 to len(parent1)-1:
    if ((i < cutpoint1) or (i >= cutpoint2)):
      offspring1[i] = find_unused(parent1, used1)
      offspring2[i] = find_unused(parent2, used2)
  # Return the two children as an array.
  return [offspring1, offspring1]
```

This code is very similar to the repeating version. The primary difference is the addition of the function **find_unused** and the two maps or dictionaries that hold a list of the elements that each child uses.

2.4.3 Other Mutation and Crossover Strategies

The algorithms provided in this chapter assume that the array lengths are fixed. This characteristic serves as a convenience rather than as a requirement of evolutionary algorithms. If you would like to use arrays of different lengths, you must implement your own crossover and mutation operators. However, you will need to perform these operations in a manner that maintains the integrity of your solutions.

Mutation tends to be an easier operation for solution arrays with differing lengths. Because mutation is asexual, you do not need to worry about how to manage two parents of differing lengths. To achieve the mutation, you just need to design the mutation operator so that it can handle arrays of variable length.

Crossover becomes much more complex when handling differing solution array lengths. Producing viable offspring array might be very difficult when performing crossover between an array of size 10 and another solution of size 10,000. Biology also has this issue. Producing viable offspring between a whale and plankton would also be difficult. Chapter 5, "Speciation," will introduce some techniques to keep incompatible individuals from attempting crossover.

NEAT, HyperNEAT and HyperNEAT ES are all examples of variable-length models that can still perform crossover (Stanley, 2009). The NEAT variants use speciation to accomplish crossover. Additionally, they employ an innovation table to allow mapping between common parts of the differing length solution array. Genetic programming utilizes trees to encode solutions. Ultimately, cutting and grafting sections of the trees brings crossover to completion (Koza, 1992).

2.5 Why is Elitism Necessary?

I will now show you an example of what can happen without elitism, a configuration setting that specifies how many of the top scoring members of a population should be passed directly into the next generation. Elitism prevents the best score from going backwards. I will show an example where the top score for a population decreases between generations 100 and 101. This can be seen in Figure 2.3.

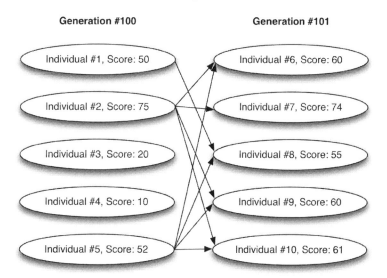

Figure 2.3: Score Degrades without Elitism

As you can see from the diagram, we cover generations 100 to 101. In the process, we can observe several developments. The selection algorithm did not pick individuals #3 and #4 for either mutation or crossover. As a result, individuals #3 and #4 did not contribute to the next generation. Their low scores most likely factored in their omission. Individual #2 demonstrated that monogamy typically does not exist in evolutionary algorithms. It mated with several different individuals and produced several offspring in generation 101.

Unfortunately, despite all the sexual and asexual births that resulted from generation 100, no children could beat individual #2's score of 75. The new best score was 74. Copying individual #2 to the next generation at the outset could have prevented this dismal outcome. Elitism is the action of making that copy.

2.6 Chapter Summary

This chapter presented three fundamental evolutionary operators: crossover, mutation, and elitism, which are the only ways that the next generation adds new members. Elitism essentially clones a highly scored individual for the next generation. Mutation asexually creates a new organism that is a slight alteration of the parent. Crossover uses sexual reproduction to create offspring that share traits of the parents.

You can implement mutation and crossover in many ways. When choosing an algorithm, you need to consider the length of your solution array. If it is variable, then you have to implement specialized versions of crossover and mutation. You must also determine if your solution array's values are numerical, categorical, or a mix of the two.

The last two chapters introduced you to the building blocks of evolutionary algorithms. In Chapter 1, you learned how algorithms create, score, and select populations. This chapter showed you how to create new population individuals using highly scored individuals. The next chapter will show you how to put these concepts all together to create an actual evolutionary algorithm.

2.6 Chapter Summary

Chapter 3

Genetic Algorithms

- Discrete Problems
- Traveling Salesman Problem (TSP)
- Continuous Problems

The first two chapters of this book defined evolutionary algorithms in a somewhat abstract sense. Scoring, selection, populations, crossover, and mutation are all critical features of evolutionary algorithms. However, we have yet to incorporate all of these features into a concrete algorithm.

Genetic algorithms are a special class of evolutionary algorithm. However, definitions vary in the body of literature that describes them. This book defines a genetic algorithm as an evolutionary algorithm that optimizes a fixed-length vector using the operators of crossover and mutation. A scoring function can then distinguish superior from inferior solutions in order to optimize the fixed-length array. This definition illustrates the essence of a genetic algorithm.

Furthermore, optional features can be added to genetic algorithms in an effort to enhance their performance. Additional techniques like speciation, elitism, and other selection methods can sometimes improve the operation of a genetic algorithm.

3.1 Genetic Algorithms for Discrete Problems

Similar to other algorithms, genetic algorithms employ slightly different approaches for continuous and discrete learning. Continuous learning deals with calculating numeric values, whereas discrete learning deals with recognizing non-numeric values. I will show you how to apply these two classic AI problems for discrete and continuous learning:

- Traveling Salesman Problem
- Iris Species Modeling

The traveling salesman problem (TSP) will show how to apply a genetic algorithm to a discrete combinational problem–the goal is to find an optimal sequence of cities. Fitting the weights of an RBF neural network for iris flower species identification will serve as the continuous problem example–the numeric weights will be adjusted.

3.1.1 The Traveling Salesman Problem (TSP)

This problem involves determining the shortest route for a traveling salesman who must visit a certain number of cities. Although he can begin and end in any city, he may visit each city only once. The TSP has several variants, some of which allow multiple visits to cities or assign different values to cities. The TSP in this chapter simply seeks the shortest possible route to visit each city one time. Figure 3.1 shows the TSP problem featured in Chapter 3 as well as the shortest route.

3.1 Genetic Algorithms for Discrete Problems

Figure 3.1: The Traveling Salesman

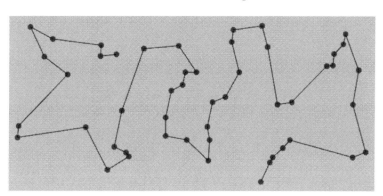

Finding the shortest route may seem like an easy task for a normal iterative program. However, as the number of cities increases, the number of possible combinations increases drastically. If the problem has one or two cities, only one or two routes are possible. If it includes three cities, the possible routes increase to six. The following list shows how quickly the number of paths grows:

```
1  city   has  1 path
2  cities have 2 path
3  cities have 6 paths
4  cities have 24 paths
5  cities have 120 paths
6  cities have 720 paths
7  cities have 5,040 paths
8  cities have 40,320 paths
9  cities have 362,880 paths
10 cities have 3,628,800 paths
11 cities have 39,916,800 paths
12 cities have 479,001,600 paths
13 cities have 6,227,020,800 paths
...
50 cities have 3.041 * 10^64 paths
```

In the above table, the formula to calculate total paths is the factorial. The number of cities, n, is calculated using the factorial operator (*!*). The factorial of some arbitrary value n is given by $n * (n - 1) * (n - 2) * ... * 3 * 2 * 1$. These values become incredibly large when a program must do a *brute-force* search. The traveling salesman problem is an example of a non-deterministic polynomial time (NP) hard problem. Informally, NP-hard is defined as any problem that lacks an efficient way to verify a correct solution. The TSP fits this definition for more than 10 cities. A formal definition of NP-hard can be found in the book *Computers and Intractability: A Guide to the Theory of NP-Completeness* (Garey, 1979).

Dynamic programming is another common approach to the traveling salesman problem, as seen in xkcd.com comic in Figure 3.2.

Figure 3.2: The Traveling Salesman (from xkcd.com)

Although this book does not include a full discussion of dynamic programming, understanding its essential function is valuable. Dynamic programming breaks a large problem, like the TSP, into smaller problems. Work can be reused for many of the smaller programs, thereby decreasing the amount of iterations required by a brute-force solution.

Unlike brute-force solutions and dynamic programming, a genetic algorithm is not guaranteed to find the best solution. Although it will find a good solution, the score might not be the best. The sample program examined in the next section shows how a genetic algorithm produced an acceptable solution for the 50-city problem in a matter of minutes (Behzad, 2002).

3.1.2 Designing a Genetic Algorithm for the TSP

TSP is one of most famous computer science problems. As an NP-hard problem that traditional iterative algorithms cannot generally solve, programmers can use genetic algorithms to generate potential solutions. Therefore, we will study how to apply a genetic algorithm to the TSP.

A discrete genetic algorithm dictates the type of crossover and mutation operators that you will use. Since a discrete problem is categorical, you will not be dealing with numbers. Thus, the cities that you might visit are the categorical information in the TSP. The list of cities, in the order of the visits, is the genome for each solution. The following shows how you might express a TSP genome:

```
[Los Angles, Chicago, New York]
```

Your initial population will be random permutations of these cities. For example, an initial random population might look like the following list:

```
[Los Angles, Chicago, New York]
[Chicago, Los Angles, New York]
[New York, Los Angles, Chicago]
```

You can create a scoring function for the above cities by calculating the miles traveled over each path. Consider the first population member. Los Angeles to Chicago is 2,016 miles, according to the programming language R's *ggmap* package. Chicago to New York is 790 miles. Therefore, the entire distance that the first population member covers is 2,806. The distance is the score that we want to minimize. The above three population members are shown here with their scores.

```
[Los Angles, Chicago, New York] -> Score: 2,016 + 790 = 2,806
[Chicago, Los Angles, New York] -> Score: 2,016 + 2,776 = 4,792
[New York, Los Angles, Chicago] -> Score: 2,776 + 2,016 = 4,792
```

As you can see, the last two paths have the same score. Because the salesman can start in any city, the last two paths produce the same distance. Some variants of the traveling salesman problem fix the starting and ending cities. As the traveling salesman's home city, the starting and ending points are identical. Other variants allow the salesman to visit the same city more than once. In short, how you define the rules for the traveling salesman problem determines how you implement the computer program.

Consider the scenario in which the traveling salesman always starts and returns to the same city–his home city. In this example, the home city is St. Louis, MO. Furthermore, the score will be the cheapest airfare. Since the genome will still consist of permutations of Los Angles, Chicago and New York, it is not necessary for St. Louis to appear at the beginning and end of the genome. This prevents the algorithm from changing St. Louis as the beginning or ending point of the path. In other words, the score function implicitly recognizes St Louis as the starting point and final destination and handles it appropriately. Examine the first population member, shown here.

```
[Los Angles, Chicago, New York]
```

The example includes the following legs of the journey:

```
St. Louis to Los Angles -> Fare: $393
Los Angles to Chicago -> Fare: $452
Chicago to New York -> Fare: $248
New York to St. Louis -> Fare: $295
Total: $1388
```

This small change to the problem introduces a number of complexities. Because St. Louis is in the center of the USA, the salesman can no longer travel a simple path from east to west or west to east. Additionally, the airfares are not transposable because the fare from Chicago to St. Louis is not necessarily the same as the fare from St. Louis to Chicago. The changing price of airfare for the travel day complicates this problem even more. So, the genome could include the starting and ending days. In this way, the genetic algorithm could optimize the travel schedule as well as the order of the cities.

3.1 Genetic Algorithms for Discrete Problems

You can also create the algorithm to allow the salesman to visit the same city more than once. This requirement, though, adds more complexity to the scoring function. However, if you relax the requirement so that the salesman can visit the same city more than once, the best score will likely result from the following solution:

[Chicago, Chicago, Chicago]

The above solution is optimal. The algorithm chose the path from St. Louis to the cheapest destination–Chicago. The algorithm then chose Chicago again for the second and third stops. Since the airfare from Chicago to Chicago is $0, the score for this trip would be excellent. Obviously, in this scenario, the algorithm did no extra work for the programmer. Therefore, the scoring function needs to be more complex in order to communicate the parameters of a truly optimal solution. Perhaps some cities are more valuable and require visits while others are optional. Designing the scoring function is critical to genetic algorithm programming.

3.1.3 Application of the TSP to a Genetic Algorithm

Now we will see an example of a simple genetic algorithm with a good path through a series of cities. Fifty cities were randomly placed on a 256x256 grid. The program used a population of 1,000 paths to evolve the best path through the cities. Because the list of cities is categorical, TSP is a discrete problem. In this example, the scoring function calculates the total distance covered by a path of cities, none of which will be visited twice.

These parameters dictate the selection of the most appropriate mutation and crossover operators. For this example, a shuffle mutation operator is the best choice. As discussed in Chapter 2, a shuffle mutation operator works well with fixed-length categorical data. Likewise, we will use a non-repeating splice crossover operator. Both of operators will allow the population of 1,000 paths to evolve, and the non-repeating crossover enforces our requirement to visit the same city only once.

I ran this program through several hundred iterations until 50 iterations had passed without a single occurrence of improvement to the best path length. One iteration is the passage of a single generation. The output from the program is listed below.

```
Iteration: 1, Best Path Length = 5308.0
Iteration: 2, Best Path Length = 5209.0
Iteration: 3, Best Path Length = 5209.0
Iteration: 4, Best Path Length = 5209.0
Iteration: 5, Best Path Length = 5209.0
Iteration: 6, Best Path Length = 5163.0
Iteration: 7, Best Path Length = 5163.0
Iteration: 8, Best Path Length = 5163.0
Iteration: 9, Best Path Length = 5163.0
Iteration: 10, Best Path Length = 5163.0
...
Iteration: 260, Best Path Length = 4449.0
Iteration: 261, Best Path Length = 4449.0
Iteration: 262, Best Path Length = 4449.0
Iteration: 263, Best Path Length = 4449.0
Iteration: 264, Best Path Length = 4449.0
Iteration: 265, Best Path Length = 4449.0
Good solution found:
22>1>37>30>11>33>39>24>9>16>40>3>17>49>31>48>46>20>13>47>23>
0>2>29>27>14>34>26>15>7>35>19>21>18>6>28>25>45>8>38>43>32>
41>5>10>4>44>36>12>42
```

As you can see, 265 iterations occurred before the program settled on a solution. Because the cities are random, they do not have actual names. Instead, the cities are labeled as "1", "2", "3", and so on. The best solution, shown above, started in city 22, continued to city 1 and ultimately stopped in city 42. You can see an online TSP implementation at the following URL:

http://www.heatonresearch.com/fun/tsp/genetic

3.2 Genetic Algorithms for Continuous Problems

Programmers can also utilize genetic algorithms to evolve continuous, or numeric, data. In the following example, we will predict the type of an iris species based on four input measurements. So, our genetic algorithm will train an RBF network model.

A model is a type of algorithm that makes predictions based on an input vector. This is called predictive modeling. For the iris data set, we will provide the RBF network with four measurements that describe an iris flower. The RBF network will then predict the species of the iris species from these four measurements. It learns to make predictions by training with the 150 flowers in the example. Then the model can predict new flowers that were not included in the training set.

Let's review how to train a model. Three primary components define how the genetic algorithms train any model:

- Training settings
- Hyper-parameters
- Parameters

The training settings are unique to the genetic algorithm. Some examples are the population size, the elitism count, the crossover algorithm, and the mutation algorithm. Later in this book, we will learn particle swarm optimization (PSO) and ant colony optimization (ACO) as a training algorithm for RBF network models. ACO and PSO will have unique characteristics for its training settings. The programmer usually establishes the training parameters. So, selecting optimal ones might require some trial and error.

Hyper-parameters define the structure of the model. Consider Figure 3.3 that shows the structure of an RBF network.

Figure 3.3: An RBF Network

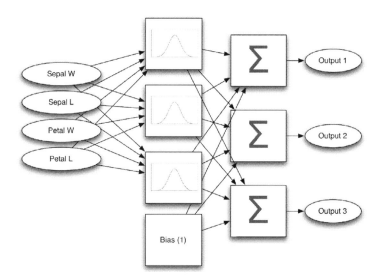

In the figure, the second column showing three boxes with bump-shaped curves are the RBF functions. They enable the RBF network to make predictions. The number of RBF networks required for this task is a hyper-parameter. The programmer or the computer can determine the hyper-parameters. Even though the RBF count does not affect genetic training, you would still need to set the RBF count if you were training with ACO or PSO. You need to be careful, though. Setting the RBF count too low will create a model that is too simple to learn the information. Setting the RBF count too high will create a network that is complex and difficult to train and may lead to overfitting, an undesirable situation where the model begins to memorize the noise in the data set rather than learning a more generalized solution. Chapter 10 will feature overfitting and the ways to avoid it in more detail. In this chapter, we will set the RBF count to 5, which seems to work well for the iris data set. I determined this number by experimentation.

3.2 Genetic Algorithms for Continuous Problems

The computer can also determine the hyper-parameters. The trial and error approach is usually the process to find them. Simply loop between 1 and 10 RBF functions and enable the computer to try each function. Once you test all 10, the program selects the model with the best score. This number will tell you the optimal settings for the RBF count hyper-parameter.

The final component is the parameter vector. As the model is trained, it adjusts the parameter vector. This aspect differs from the hyper-parameters because, once the training starts, the model does not adjust the hyper-parameters. In fact, the hyper-parameters define the model and cannot be changed. Adjusting the parameter vector is the means by which a training algorithm, such as a genetic algorithm, PSO, or ACO, teaches the model the correct response for a given input. A genetic algorithm utilizes crossover and mutation to adjust the parameter vectors.

The output listed below shows the progress of training an RBF network for the iris data set with a genetic algorithm. As you can see, the score does not improve during the first 10 iterations. Each of these iterations represents a generation of potential solutions. The score represents the percentage of the 150 iris flowers that were classified incorrectly. We seek to minimize this score.

```
Iteration #1, Score=0.1752302452792032, Species Count: 1
Iteration #2, Score=0.1752302452792032, Species Count: 1
Iteration #3, Score=0.1752302452792032, Species Count: 1
Iteration #4, Score=0.1752302452792032, Species Count: 1
Iteration #5, Score=0.1752302452792032, Species Count: 1
Iteration #6, Score=0.1752302452792032, Species Count: 1
Iteration #7, Score=0.1752302452792032, Species Count: 1
Iteration #8, Score=0.1752302452792032, Species Count: 1
Iteration #9, Score=0.1752302452792032, Species Count: 1
Iteration #10, Score=0.1752302452792032, Species Count: 1
...
Iteration #945, Score=0.05289116605845716, Species Count: 1
Iteration #946, Score=0.05289116605845716, Species Count: 1
Iteration #947, Score=0.05289116605845716, Species Count: 1
Iteration #948, Score=0.051833695704776035, Species Count: 1
Iteration #949, Score=0.05050776383877834, Species Count: 1
Iteration #950, Score=0.04932340367757065, Species Count: 1
Final score: 0.04932340367757065
[-0.55, 0.24, -0.86, -0.91] -> Iris-setosa, Ideal: Iris-setosa
```

```
[ -0.66 ,  -0.16 , -0.86 , -0.91] -> Iris-setosa , Ideal: Iris-setosa
[ -0.77 ,   0.0  , -0.89 , -0.91] -> Iris-setosa , Ideal: Iris-setosa
...
[ 0.22 , -0.16, 0.42, 0.58] -> Iris-virginica , Ideal: Iris-virginica
[ 0.05 ,  0.16, 0.49, 0.83] -> Iris-virginica , Ideal: Iris-virginica
[ -0.11, -0.16, 0.38, 0.41] -> Iris-virginica , Ideal: Iris-
    virginica
```

In the listing, you might have also observed a species count. Since we are not currently working with species, the type stays at 1. Chapter 5 will introduce species.

3.3 Other Applications of Genetic Algorithms

The iris data set and traveling salesman problem are common examples in artificial intelligence literature. Observing how various algorithms solve the same problem can be beneficial in understanding their differences. However, it is equally valuable to examine the ways in which new problems conform to the genetic algorithms. This section will show how a variety of problems might be adapted to a genetic algorithm.

Although the book does not currently implement these applications, I might include them in the future. The main purpose of the following sections is to demonstrate the application of genetic algorithms to a variety of situations.

3.3.1 Tag Clouds

Tag clouds are a convenient tool to visualize word frequency counts in a document. In fact, a small tag cloud can represent common words from a very long document. However, tag cloud algorithms typically remove structural words, such as *the*, from the word counts. Figure 3.4 features a tag cloud created from the text of *Artificial Intelligence for Humans, Volume 1: Fundamental Algorithms*.

3.3 Other Applications of Genetic Algorithms

Figure 3.4: A Tag Cloud of Volume 1

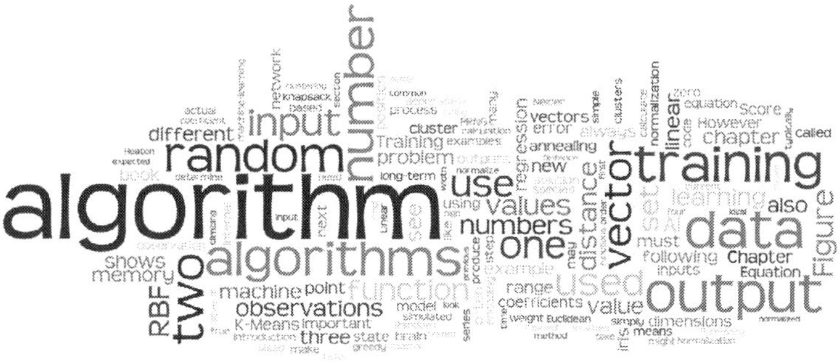

The above tag cloud shows how often each word occurs. You can easily see that "algorithm" is the most common word in the book.

To create a tag cloud, you must build a histogram of the word counts. The histogram for the above tag cloud is shown here.

```
341 algorithm
239 training
203 data
201 output
198 random
192 algorithms
169 number
163 input
...
```

The word counts provide the frequency of each word in relation to others. The words in the tag cloud are also interlocked in order to minimize the amount of white space between the words. In the example, the smaller words fill in the spaces under the *n* and *m* of *algorithm*.

To create a tag cloud, the first step is to choose the words and determine their size. The above histogram illustrates this step. Most likely, you will include about 100 of the most frequent words from the document in the tag cloud. The exact number of words in the tag cloud will be adjusted for display aesthetics. The number of times that the word appears in the text will dictate the size of the word.

Eliminating the white space is a great application for a genetic algorithm. The x and y coordinates, serving as an orientation, represent each word and specify the location of each word on the display. The orientation dictates whether the word is horizontal or vertical. These three data items produce a vector equal to three times the number of words in the tag cloud. If you displayed 100 words, then the vector would be 300 elements long. The score would penalize the genome for both the white space and the overlapping text. Tag clouds should never have overlapping text. Therefore, you need to create a score function similar to the following:

```
[white space pixels] + ( [overlapping pixels] * 100)
```

The genetic algorithm should seek to minimize this score function. If the text overlaps, you need to increase the *100* coefficient.

3.3.2 Mosaic Art

Art generation is another very common example of genetic algorithms. Writing a scoring function for computer art is very easy. You simply compare the source image to the one created by the genetic algorithm. You also provide the genetic algorithm with a set of tools so that it can produce an image and display its simulated creativity.

A human painter works the same way. Obviously, the easiest way for the painter to produce an image would be to photograph his subject with a digital camera. However, he creates art with his set of tools-a brush and paint. For the genetic algorithm, the tools are the graphical commands of a programming language. The scoring function simply compares the original image to what the genetic algorithm produced. For example, you could limit the genetic algorithm so that it draws circles with only a handful of colors. The genetic algorithm would evolve to produce the best possible rendition of the original photograph, using just the elements that it was allowed in the program. In this way, it displays its simulated creativity.

One example of computer art that you can create with a genetic algorithm is a mosaic, which is a large image composed of a collection of smaller images. The master image contains an imaginary grid. Then smaller images are placed in each grid cell. Figure 3.5 shows a mosaic.

3.3 Other Applications of Genetic Algorithms

Figure 3.5: Wynton the Cockatiel as a Mosaic

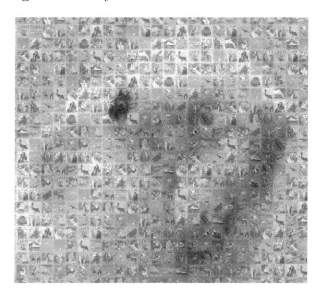

The above image depicts a cockatiel created from a mosaic of animal pictures. To create this mosaic, the image of a cockatiel was 2,048 by 2,048 pixels. A grid of smaller animal pictures, each 32x32 pixels, would make up the mosaic. If you overlay a grid of these smaller animal images onto the large image, you would have a 64x64 grid. Choose the set of the smaller animal pictures to place into the 64x64 grid that would create a grid most like the one of my pet cockatiel.

Each genome would be a fixed-length array with a length equal to 64 multiplied 64, or 4,096 bytes. Each genome would be of length 4,096. Use a scoring function to compare the difference between the generated mosaic grid image and the original. Once the scoring is minimized, you would have a mosaic that closely resembles the cockatiel.

3.4 Chapter Summary

Genetic algorithms utilize populations, scoring, crossover, and mutation to solve actual programming problems. Genetic algorithms are the concrete implementation of the concepts learned in Chapters 1 and 2. They work with crossover and mutation to evolve better solutions over subsequent generations.

Genetic algorithms require that solutions be represented as a fixed-length array. This requirement might seem limiting, but many solutions can be represented this way. In this chapter, I also demonstrated the traveling salesman problem and the iris data set. Additionally, I discussed how genetic algorithms could be applied to tag clouds and image mosaics.

To progress beyond fixed-length arrays, the next chapter will demonstrate how to evolve actual programs. In fact, genetic programming can represent a computer program as a tree structure in order to create better programs for the next generation.

3.4 Chapter Summary

Chapter 4

Genetic Programming

- Programs as Trees
- Generating Trees
- Crossover and Mutation for Trees
- Fitting Equations

Chapter 3 presented genetic algorithms that work with a solution array of a fixed length. However, computer programs are versatile and can represent solutions in different ways. Of these possibilities, genetic programming allows you to encode solutions as evolving programs to solve problems.

Unfortunately, the computer cannot simply evolve a Python or C# application. Genetic programming requires you to encode your program in a very specific format. As a result, trees can represent computer programs. Since this concept is basic computer science, you might already be familiar with this representation. In any case, we will review tree representation in the next section.

4.1 Programs as Trees

Mathematical expressions are a basic component of computer programs. We will begin by exploring the various ways to represent a mathematical expression as a tree. You will often see an expression written as Equation 4.1.

$$\sqrt{\frac{3}{4}x^2 - 1} \qquad (4.1)$$

This example is a very common and standardized way of representing an equation. For instance, given that the value of **x** is 5, you could provide the answer. If you are a programmer, you might prefer Equation 4.1 written as program code.

```
print(   sqrt(0.75*pow(x,2))-1 )
```

The function **pow**, in case you are not familiar with it, raises the first argument to the power of the second.

An important point of both of these encodings is precedence. The rules of precedence tell you that if x is 5, then you raise 5 to the power of 2, yielding 25. You do not multiply 5 by 0.75, yielding 0.375, and then take 0.375 to the power of 2. Exponent operators have higher precedence than multiplication operators. The above code clarifies this idea better than Equation 4.1. Looking at the code, a programmer would easily understand the mathematical order and evaluate **pow(x,2)** before the next step because functions always go first. A function call within another function call always evaluates the inner function first. Consider the following code:

```
print( sqrt(pow(x,2)) )
```

Here, the program must evaluate **pow** first. That result is subsequently passed to **sqrt**.

4.1 Programs as Trees

In isolation, functions are not ambiguous, and they don't require any rules of precedence. However, operators are ambiguous when they lack rules of precedence. The following formula illustrates this ambiguity:

```
3+5*2
```

What is the value of the above formula? Can you determine the value by multiplying 5 by 2 and then adding the answer to 3? Or do you obtain the value by adding 3 to 5 and then multiplying by 2? The two processes give you different answers. Of course, precedence dictates that multiplication goes before addition. However, the process loses its ambiguity as soon as you use functions instead of operators. After all, operators are just shorthand for functions. There is no difference between *2*3* and *mult(2,3)*.

Consider the above expression written with only functions.

```
add(3,mult(5,2))
```

If you are dealing with only functions, you do not need to know any rules of precedence. The grouping parentheses are not required either. Equation 4.1 shows code that contains only functions.

```
print( sub(sqrt(mult(0.75,pow(x,2))),1) )
```

The above statement requires no knowledge of precedence because the order is completely unambiguous. The programming language LISP represents expressions this way using s-expressions. The above code, translated to a LISP s-expression, appears as follows:

```
(- (sqrt (* 0.75 (expt x 2 ) ) ) 1 )
```

Notice that LISP calls functions in the following form:

```
([function_name] arg1 arg2 etc)
```

In LISP, you write 5+6 as the following:

```
(+ 5 6)
```

4.1.1 Postfix Notation

Postfix notation is another way to represent expressions. It is often referred to as reverse Polish notation (RPN). Equation 4.1 could be represented as the following postfix notation expression:

```
0.75 x 2 pow * sqrt 1 -
```

This expression can be treated as a stack. Evaluate its parts from left to right, pushing each onto a stack. Initially, place the 0.75 on the stack.

```
0.75
```

Next, place the value held by the variable **x** on the stack.

```
5
0.75
```

Following the postfix expression, place 2 on the stack.

```
2
5
0.75
```

Because we have not yet added a function, we still cannot process anything on the stack. However, once we place **pow**, a function that requires two arguments, on the stack, we can remove two arguments off the stack and perform **pow** on them. This process results in taking 5 to the power of 2, which is the value 25. Thus, we put 25 on the stack to replace the two arguments.

```
25
0.75
```

Next, we place the **multiply** opcode on the stack. Because multiply is a function that accepts two arguments, we remove the two arguments from the stack and perform multiplication. This process results in 0.75 times 25, or 18.75. We now have a single value for the stack.

```
18.75
```

4.1 Programs as Trees

Next, we place the **sqrt** function on the stack. The **sqrt** function accepts a single argument and returns the square root. The value 18.75 is popped from the stack, and we use it to calculate the square root to be 4.33.

```
4.33
```

Now we push the value 1 on the stack.

```
1
4.33
```

Lastly, we process the final subtract operator, which subtracts 1 from 4.33, giving us 3.33.

```
3.33
```

We now have a single value on the stack. Since we are at the end of our prefix expression, no further values remain to add to the stack. We are done; the answer is 3.33.

4.1.2 Tree Notation

As you noticed from the previous section, a variety of ways exists to write the same expression. In this section, I will show you one final way to write the above expression–tree notation. Consider the postfix notation from the previous section.

```
0.75 x 2 pow * sqrt 1 -
```

Figure 4.1 demonstrates the way you write the notation.

Figure 4.1: A Tree Expression

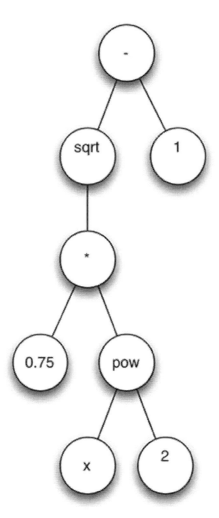

As you can see, subtraction is the root node, which is the top node without parents. The root node is always the node whose operation is performed last. All of the other functions must be performed before we can perform the subtraction. Thus, the root node always appears last in prefix notation.

4.1.3 Terminal and Non-terminal Nodes

Each of the circles in Figure 4.1 is a node with a certain number of connections. The type of node dictates the connection count. For example, multiplication will always have two connections, or arguments. Similarly, square root will always have a single connection. The variables (e.g., x) and constants never have connections.

The presence or absence of connections divides the node types into two very high-level groups. The first classification occurs when a node has no connections. Its classification is terminal because nothing comes after it. The other grouping is non-terminal nodes, which can perform operations on the terminal nodes. For example, the non-terminal node "addition" would perform the addition operation on two terminal nodes that hold the constants 5 and 10. This process would give the "addition" node the value of 15.

Most genetic programming algorithms are implemented to create a constant pool (Koza, 1992). A constant pool is simply a fixed list of unique constant values for the genetic program to use. Most programming languages utilize constant pools by first scanning the source code for unique constant values and building them into a list.

The program in Figure 4.1 has three different constants: 0.75, 1 and 2. When the genetic programming algorithm is first started, it creates a pool of random constants. The size of the constant pool is a hyper-parameter to the genetic program. However, the program never adds new constants to this pool. In other words, the size of the pool has to be sufficient for the existing constants. Ensuring that the pool has several important numbers, such as 0.5, 1, 2, 10 and 100, is also good practice. If you think your solution might need certain numeric constants, you may also add those numbers. Through various combinations of addition, subtraction, multiplication, and division operators, the pool will allow your program to evolve these extra but required constants.

4.1.4 Evaluating Trees

Recursion facilitates tree expression evaluation. A simple tree evaluator is shown in Listing 4.1.

Listing 4.1: Evaluating Trees

```
sub eval(node)
# First, handle regular opcodes, these are binary (two arguments)
  if node.type == ADD:
    return eval(node.child[0]) + eval(node.child[1])
  elif node.type == SUBTRACT:
    return eval(node.child[0]) - eval(node.child[1])
  elif node.type == DIVIDE:
    return eval(node.child[0]) / eval(node.child[1])
  elif node.type == MULTIPLY:
    return eval(node.child[0]) * eval(node.child[1])
# Now, handle unary (single argument)
  elif node.type == NEGATE:
    return -eval(node.child[0])
  elif node.type == SQRT:
    return sqrt(eval(node.child[0]))
  else
# Now, handle variable and constant opcodes,
# these are terminal (no arguments)
    index = node.type - VAR_CONST
    if index >= len(const_values) + len(var_values):
      throw error("Invalid opcode: " + node.type)
    if index < len(var_values):
      return var_values[index]
    else
      return const_values[index - this.varCount]
```

The above code shows that the program provides a variable called **node** to the function named **eval**. This function will evaluate all branches below node and return a floating-point number. If you would like to evaluate the entire tree, pass the root node to **eval**. As you can see, **eval** recursively calls itself. For example, if you call **eval** for an **ADD** node, **eval** will be called for each of the two child nodes. The two operands for the addition are the two child nodes for **ADD**.

4.1 Programs as Trees

Each node has an opcode. The opcode tells the node to perform a particular function. Opcodes represent functions such as addition, subtraction, division, multiplication, negation, and square root. Opcodes also represent variables (such as **x**) and constants (such as 3.5).

The **ADD**, **SUBTRACT**, **DIVIDE** and **MULTIPLY** opcodes are all binary because they take two arguments. The **NEGATE** and **SQRT** opcodes are both unary because they take a single argument. The negation is simply a leading negative sign, such as **-x**. The single argument for the negation is the value to flip between negative and positive.

Finally, we evaluate the terminal nodes. Any node that has an opcode greater than **VAR_CONST** is considered to be a terminal node, which has no arguments and represents the variables and the constants. You can visualize all of the opcodes in Figure 4.2.

Figure 4.2: Typical Opcode Layout for Simple Expressions

#	Opcode	Purpose
0	ADD	Addition (two arguments)
1	SUBTRACT	Subtraction (two arguments)
2	MULTIPLY	Multiplication (two arguments)
3	DIVIDE	Division (two arguments)
4	NEGATE	Negate (one argument)
5	SQRT	Square root (one argument)
6	VAR_CONST + 0	First variable (e.g. x)
7	VAR_CONST + 1	Second variable (e.g. y)
8	VAR_CONST + 2	First constant (e.g. 1)
9	VAR_CONST + 3	Second constant (e.g. 2)
10	VAR_CONST + 4	Third constant (e.g. 0.5)

Opcodes 0 through 5 handle the binary and unary functions. The opcode **VAR_CONST** defines the storage location of the variables and constants. Figure 4.2 has two variables (x & y), as well as three constants. By convention, the variables precede the constants.

The terms opcode and node can be used interchangeably. The node is the tree element that contains the opcode and any children. The opcode is simply an integer that defines the operation that the node will perform. This operation will be performed in conjunction with the node's children that contain the opcode.

4.1.5 Generating Trees

Like other evolutionary algorithms, genetic programming starts with a random population. This process is simply a matter of generating a number of random individuals equal to the desired population count. You can use several popular algorithms to produce a random individual. I will discuss these algorithms in the next sections.

Additionally, several training settings and hyper-parameters influence the way the population is created. They are the following:

- **Population size** is the fixed population size. The initial population will be this size.

- **Constant pool size** is the number of constant opcodes that will be available.

- **Low-constant range** is the low-end of the range for constant pool member generation.

- **High-constant range** is the high-end of the range for constant pool member generation.

- **Maximum depth** is the greatest depth that a random tree can attain.

- **Tree Initialization algorithm** is the method that generates the initial population of random trees.

There is also a variable count that is part of the problem definition. For a simple equation that only uses **x**, the variable count would be 1. For the iris data set, the variable count would be 4 in order to match the iris measurements.

4.1 Programs as Trees

The constant pool size and constant pool range are both considered hyperparameters because they define the nature of the model. You cannot change the constant pool values training since this change would affect the numeric values that your model needs for calculation.

The maximum depth and tree initialization algorithm are both training settings. These values affect only the node structure of the initial trees from the population. In other words, the program does not use them beyond training and the initial population generation.

Most tree initialization algorithms begin by creating a root node. Then they add nodes to the root. To accomplish this process, we first need to select a root node type. We can choose from different sets of opcodes to select a random node.

- **All node types** - This set includes all available opcodes, no matter if they are a function, variable, or constant.

- **Function nodes** - This set contains all function opcodes. If an opcode has children, it belongs in this set.

- **Terminal nodes** - This set has the variable and constant opcodes. If an opcode does not have children, it belongs in this set.

The different population initialization algorithms will use these three sets.

4.1.6 Full Tree Initialization

One of the earliest initialization algorithms developed for genetic programming was the full tree initialization algorithm (Koza, 1992). The pseudocode for full tree initialization is shown in Listing 4.2.

Listing 4.2: Generate a Population with the Full Algorithm

```
# Recursive full function.  If we still have
# remaining depth, then generate a function node
# and continue recursive descent to children.
sub full_node(remaining_depth):
  # If there is still depth, create a function.
  # Functions have children and will continue.
```

```
if remaining_depth >0:
    this_node = choose_function_node()
else:
# If no depth remains, then create a terminal node.
# Terminal nodes have no children, and will stop.
    this_node = choose_terminal_node()

# Generate the required number of children.
# This is zero for terminal nodes.
for i from 1 to this_node.needed_children
    this_node.add(full_node(remaining_depth-1))
# Generate a full population.
sub full_population(population_size, max_depth):
    population = new Population()

    for i from 1 to population_size:
        population.add(full_node(max_depth))

    return population
```

As you can see, the above code uses recursion to create a tree. Figure 4.3 shows how a full tree might be generated.

Figure 4.3: Full Tree Initialization

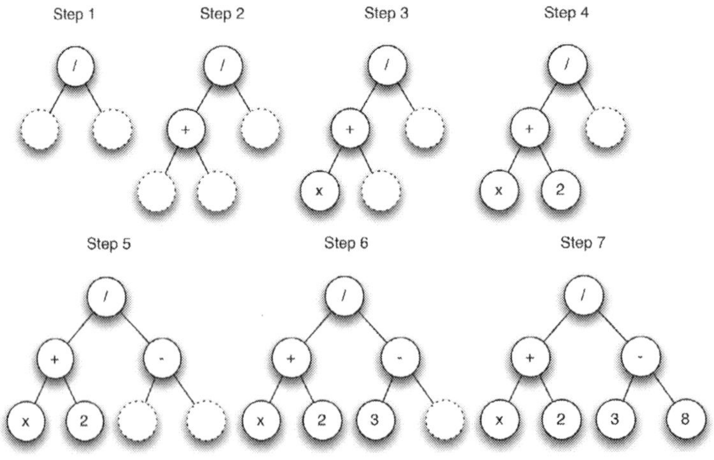

We specify a maximum tree depth of 3. A quick look at the final step 7 shows us that the tree was created with a depth of 2. The tree is depth

4.1 Programs as Trees

2 because two edges (the lines) between the terminal node and the root are present.

Step 1 begins by generating the root node. We are not yet at the final layer, so we choose a random function node for the root. Because we chose the divide opcode, we now have two child nodes to fill.

Step 2 chooses a random function for the first child of the root. An *add* opcode is chosen. Because we are not yet at the maximum depth, we choose another random function opcode. We now have two more child nodes to fill.

For step 3, we now fill the first child of the *add* opcode. Since this child is at the maximum depth, we choose a random terminal opcode, which will stop the tree from proceeding deeper. Step 4 performs a similar operation for the second child of the *add* opcode. The tree is now partially filled to the terminal nodes. The remaining steps continue in a similar fashion.

4.1.7 Grow Tree Initialization

Another early initialization algorithm developed for genetic programming was the grow tree initialization algorithm (Koza, 1992). Its pseudocode is shown in Listing 4.3.

Listing 4.3: Generate a Population with the Grow Algorithm

```
# Recursive grow function. If we still have
# remaining depth, then generate a function node
# and continue recursive descent to children.
sub grow_node(remaining_depth):
  # If there is still depth, create a node.
  # Functions have children and will continue.
  if remaining_depth >0:
    this_node = choose_node()
  else:
  # If no depth remains, then create a terminal node.
  # Terminal nodes have no children, and will stop.
    this_node = choose_terminal_node()

  # Generate the required number of children.
  # This is zero for terminal nodes.
  for i from 1 to this_node.needed_children
```

```
      this_node.add(full_node(remaining_depth-1))
# Generate a grow population.
sub grow_population(population_size, max_depth):
  population = new Population()

  for i from 1 to population_size:
    population.add(grow_node(max_depth))

  return population
```

As you can see, the above code uses recursion to create a tree. Figure 4.4 shows how a grow tree might be generated.

Figure 4.4: Grow Tree Initialization

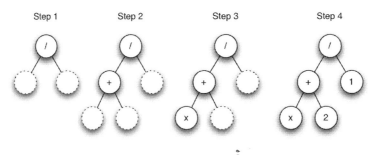

The grow algorithm works very similar to the full algorithm. The primary differences are that the grow algorithm does not require that nodes be function opcodes before reaching the final level. Step 1 begins by choosing the root node, which is determined from the entire set of opcodes. The algorithm happened to select a divide function opcode. If the algorithm had chosen a terminal node for the root, then the tree would be finished, and it would have only one node.

Step 2 begins by filling one of the two child nodes for the divide node. The program can choose the two child nodes from the entire set of nodes. An add function is selected for the first child. Steps 3 and 4 show how the rest of the tree is completed. Step 4 singles out a terminal node (1) as the second child of the divide opcode. This selection causes the tree to appear off balance.

4.1.8 Ramped Half-and-Half Initialization

Neither the grow nor the full algorithm provides a wide array of shapes and depths. As a result, Koza (1992) proposed a combination called the ramped half-and-half initialization algorithm, which will create half of the initial population using full while half is constructed using grow. Additionally, it uses a range of maximum depths that provides a greater variation in tree sizes than a fixed-maximum depth. Listing 4.4 shows the ramped half-and-half algorithm.

Listing 4.4: Generate a Ramped Half-and-Half Population

```
# Generate a ramped half-and-half population.
sub grow_population(population_size, min_depth, max_depth):
  population = new Population()

  for i from 1 to population_size:
    # Generate a random depth.
    depth = random_uniform(min_depth, max_depth+1)

    # Use either grow or full with 0.5 likelihood.
    if random_uniform() > 0.5:
      population.add(grow_node(depth))
    else:
      population.add(full_node(depth))
  return population
```

The above code makes use of the **grow_node** and **full_node** methods discussed previously in this chapter. The ramped algorithm chooses between grow and full with a 50% probability. Additionally, the algorithm chooses random tree depths between the **min_depth** and **max_depth** training parameters.

4.1.9 Reservoir Sampling

Chapter 3 showed the crossover and mutation operators for fixed-length arrays. Before exploring crossover and mutation for trees, we must learn how to randomly select a node from a tree. Both crossover and mutation for fixed arrays need a method for selecting a random element in the array. The length of a fixed-length array is known by definition–it is fixed. Simply select a random number between zero and one less than the length of the array. For example, if the array length is 10, then choose a random number between 0 and 9. That random number specifies the random-array element you just chose, assuming the array starts at index zero.

Although picking a random-array element from a tree is much more difficult, you can perform this operation in several ways. An easy but inefficient method is to calculate the size of the tree, which is the number of nodes present. However, a computer does not inherently know this number, and the trees are not guaranteed to have the same sizes. As a result, a common problem arises in computer science. To determine the size of a tree, the algorithm must visit each node of the tree and count the number of nodes.

Visiting every node is tree traversal, and several algorithms exist that provide different orderings of the nodes. Because we are simply counting the nodes, the ordering is not essential. The algorithm choice does not matter either. As a result, we will choose a simple but efficient traversal algorithm. The preorder tree traversal algorithm is a good choice for node counting.

This algorithm is recursive and completes the following steps:

- Visit the root.
- Traverse sub-trees, starting at the left.
- Increase node count by 1.

Listing 4.5 shows a pseudocode implementation.

Listing 4.5: Preorder Tree Traversal

```
sub count_nodes(node):
  total_count = 1

  for child in node.children:
    total_count = total_count + count_nodes(child)

  return total_count
```

The above code returns the count of child nodes for any node that the function passes. If you execute this code for the root node, you are given the node count

4.1 Programs as Trees

for the entire tree. When the algorithm is executed for the root node, you can see that it calls itself for each of the children of the root. Because of this recursion, the **count_nodes** function will call itself for each of the children. This process continues until all the children below the starting point are visited. Figure 4.5 shows how this traversal occurs.

Figure 4.5: Preorder Tree Traversal

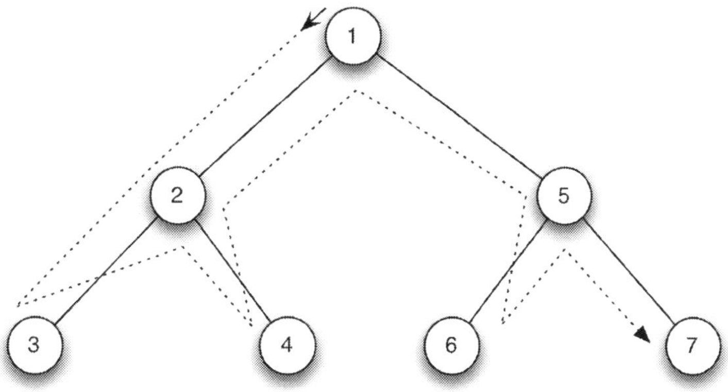

Once the algorithm has the size of the tree, it can choose a random number between zero and one less than that length to determine the desired tree nodes. We now traverse the tree a second time and stop once we've passed a quantity of nodes that equal this random number. Although this method of node selection works, it is inefficient because we must traverse the tree twice. Nevertheless, the second traversal will probably not be a full traversal.

Reservoir sampling (Vitter, 1985) is an algorithm that allows a random node to be selected without two traversals. Vitter first introduced this important concept for big data as *Algorithm R*. To understand this concept, consider how would you choose a random person from the world population. This process is complicated because you do not know the total world population when you first start meeting people. If you did, it would be easy. Just pick a random number between zero and one less than the exact world population. Now, start visiting people in any order that guarantees no repeat visits. Once you've visited a number of people equal to the random number, you have your selection.

However, you do not know the exact world population. You cannot use an estimate without introducing bias. If your estimate is too low, then your selection is biased towards people you meet first. If your estimate is too high, then your selection is biased towards people you meet last. You don't want to visit the world population twice. Indeed, you don't want to do anything twice with big data!

Reservoir sampling provides a good solution. You begin by visiting each person, keeping a candidate individual as you visit the population. The first person you visit becomes the first candidate. When you visit the second person, you generate a random number between 1 and 2. If this number is 1, then the second person becomes the new candidate. The second person has a 50% chance of being the candidate. Now you visit the third person and generate a random number between 1 and 3. If this number is 1, then the third person is the candidate, with a 33.33% chance to be selected. This process continues for all people. At the end, whoever is the candidate becomes the selection. Consequently, your selection stems from just one visit to each candidate.

The name reservoir sampling aptly reflects the selection process involved in the algorithm. The reservoir is the person you are retaining as the candidate. Sampling simply refers to the statistical process of choosing one or more individuals from the population. You can see the pseudocode for randomly choosing a tree node in Listing 4.6.

Listing 4.6: Choose a Random Tree Node with Reservoir Sampling

```
# Traverse the tree, index and reservoir are passed by reference.
sub internal_sample_node(current_node, ref index, ref reservoir):
  current_index = index
  index = index + 1
  # Determine if we replace the reservoir.
  j = random_uniform(0, current_index + 1)
  if j == 0:
    reservoir = current_node
  # Traverse on to the children.
  for child_node in current_node.children:
    internal_sample_node(child_node, index, reservoir)
# Return a random node from a tree using reservoir sampling.
sub sample_node(root):
  index = 0
  reservoir = null
```

```
    internal_sample_node(root,index,reservoir)
  return reservoir
```

The above code provides a function, which is called **sample_node,** and it will choose a random node from a tree. The root node must be passed to **sample_node**. The **sample_node** function is called **internal_sample_node**. The internal function performs a recursive traversal of the tree, using the pre-order traversal algorithm. The variables **reservoir** and **index** keep track of the current reservoir item and index, respectively. Both of these variables are passed by reference. As a result, changes to them are reflected outside of the function.

4.2 Mutating Trees

Mutation for genetic programs works in the same principle way as the genetic algorithms that we saw in Chapter 3. Both mutation algorithms implement asexual reproduction, creating offspring that are based on one randomly altered parent. You can see the pseudocode for a tree mutation in Listing 4.7.

Listing 4.7: Tree Mutate Pseudocode
```
sub tree_mutate(parent,max_mutate_depth):
  # Clone the parent.
  child = parent.clone()
  # Choose the point to mutate.
  mutate_point = sample_node(child)
  # Replace the mutate point with a new random tree section.
  child.replace(mutate_point,grow_node(max_mutate_depth))
  return child
```

First, a child is created that is an exact clone of the parent. The algorithm then chooses a random mutation point in the child. This random point is replaced with a new tree that was created with the **grow_node** function introduced earlier. We essentially cut off a branch from the child and allow a new branch to grow in its place. Figure 4.6 shows this process.

Figure 4.6: Mutation Operator for Trees

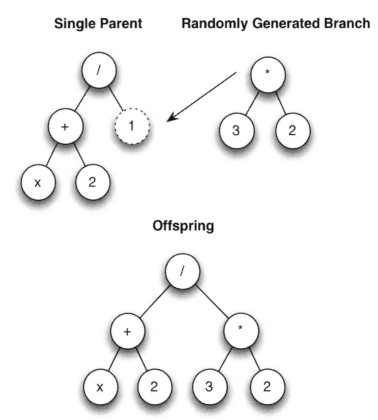

As you can see in the above picture, we choose a random point in the parent. We then generate a random branch. The child is subsequently created with the random branch grafted into the point selected on the parent. It is important to note that the parent is not altered during this operation.

4.3 Tree Crossover

Tree crossover allows two parent trees to reproduce sexually. Crossover works by copying parent 1, and then it grafts a copied portion of parent 2 into the copy of parent 1. Neither parent is altered in this process. Listing 4.8 shows the pseudocode to implement crossover.

Listing 4.8: Tree Crossover Pseudocode

```
sub tree_crossover(parent1, parent2):
  # Find a random point in parent 2,
  # we will copy this to the new child.
  source = sample_node(parent2.root)
  # Create the child as a clone of parent 1.
  child = parent1.clone()
  # Find a random point in the child to graft in parent 2 point.
  target = sample_node(child.root)
  # Replace at the child's random point with a
  #clone of parent 2's point.
  child.replace(target, source.clone())
  return child
```

Two parents, called **parent1** and **parent2**, are passed to the **tree_crossover** function. The algorithm begins by choosing a random point in **parent2**, called **source**. Next the **child** is created initially as a clone of **parent1**. A second random point, called **target**, is chosen in this newly created **child**, and a random point is chosen in the **child**, called **target**. Finally, a copy of **source** is grafted onto the child tree at point **target**. Figure 4.7 summarizes this process.

Figure 4.7: Crossover Operator for Trees

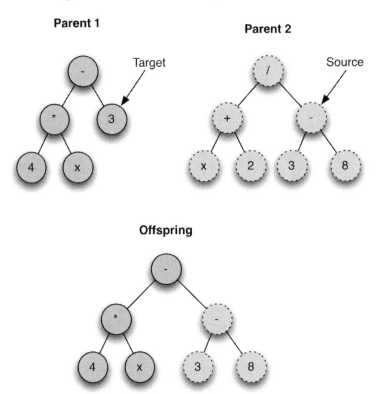

As you can see in the above figure, the algorithm chooses a target from the first parent and a source from the second parent. Copying this source to the target creates the offspring. However, neither parent is changed in the process.

4.4 Fitting Equations

The last section showed how you could represent equations as evolvable trees, which allows you to generate an equation that represents a data set. This is one of the most common uses for genetic programming. For example, consider the following data set:

```
x,y
-10,342
-9,272
-8,210
-7,156
-6,110
-5,72
-4,42
-3,20
-2,6
-1,0
0,2
1,12
2,30
3,56
4,90
5,132
6,182
7,240
8,306
9,380
10,462
```

This data set shows the value of y for various x values. This is an example of regression, rather than classification. Regression problems seek to predict a numeric outcome for a given input. For the above data set, the input is x and the outcome is y. We could use an RBF network, as seen in Chapter 3, to perform this regression. However, one problem with an RBF network is that it is not explainable.

Explainability can be very important in certain domains of AI. Your RBF model might tell you that the outcome for an x value of -5 is 72; however, it won't tell you the reason for this outcome. In this sense, an RBF network is a black box. A black box algorithm cannot explain how it comes up with an answer. Human intuition works along the same lines. Often human beings cannot explain a decision; they simply believe it is the right course of action. Black box models should not be used when the decision must be explained. In these cases, use genetic programming or one of the linear models from volume 1 of this series.

Formulas are very explainable. If I were to tell you that Equation 4.2 represents the above data set, you now know a considerable amount about the way that the outcome is determined.

$$y = 4x^2 + 6x + 2 \qquad (4.2)$$

The above equation exactly defines the relationship between x and y, and it is not necessary to query a black box model to determine other values. Genetic programming allows you to produce an equation from a data set.

We will train from the above data to determine whether the equation that we train will be similar to Equation 4.2. A sample run of this example is shown here.

```
Iteration: 1, Current error = 20710.295679925002, Best Solution
    Length = 20
Iteration: 2, Current error = 20710.295679925002, Best Solution
    Length = 20
Iteration: 3, Current error = 20710.295679925002, Best Solution
    Length = 20
Iteration: 4, Current error = 18435.519210663904, Best Solution
    Length = 16
Iteration: 5, Current error = 18435.519210663904, Best Solution
    Length = 16
...
Iteration: 996, Current error = 8.510634781265793, Best Solution
    Length = 14
Iteration: 997, Current error = 8.510634781265793, Best Solution
    Length = 14
Iteration: 998, Current error = 8.510634781265793, Best Solution
    Length = 14
Iteration: 999, Current error = 8.510634781265793, Best Solution
    Length = 14
Good solution found:
(((-(((-2.36732495)-a)-a))*(-((-0.87349794-a)-a)))
```

4.4 Fitting Equations

You can see that the example converged to an error around 8.5. It might take a few runs of the program to reach a good error. Populations can sometimes stagnate on a mediocre solution. Chapter 5, "Speciation," will show one way to prevent stagnation.

I also limited the maximum length of the tree to 50. Although different methods of limiting the tree lengths exist, I prefer to build the limitations into the scoring function. If the length of a genome is over 50, the score function returns a really bad score.

As you notice in the above output, the algorithm chose the following equation that best fit the data:

$$(((-(((-2.36732495)-a)-a))*(-((-0.87349794-a)-a)))$$

At first, this equation may not seem like an adequate solution because it is much more complex than Equation 4.2. However, the genetic algorithm does not know algebra. If we simplify the above equation, the resulting formula is Equation 4.3.

$$4a^2 + 6.48165a^2 + 2.06785 \qquad (4.3)$$

As you can see, this solution is much closer to the original equation.

You might wonder why the genetic programming algorithm was unable to figure out a simplified expression. When I first started experimenting with genetic programming, this issue intrigued me as well. I found that a genetic program would never converge to a particularly simple form because of the way that it implements mutation and crossover. Consider how Equation 4.4 could be simplified.

$$4x + 2x \qquad (4.4)$$

Figure 4.8 shows Equation 4.4 in tree form as well the simplified equation in tree form.

Figure 4.8: Simplify a Tree

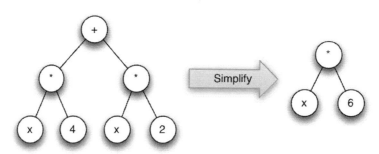

Thinking back to tree mutation and crossover, we can see why the above equation cannot easily evolve into a simplified form. Mutation works by inserting a new branch into part of the parent. No single part of the simplified tree can be replaced to form the simplified tree. This change would require several mutations before the simplification occurred. Additionally, each incremental change would severely worsen the score of the child and decrease the child's chances of selection.

Crossover would have a similar issue in creating offspring that complete the simplification shown in Figure 4.8. Grafting a branch from another parent will not produce the simplification in one generation.

Because of this issue, most genetic programs use computer algebra systems (CAS) to perform these simplifications. Once an optimal solution is found, it is better to perform these simplifications at the end. Premature simplification causes the genome to have fewer nodes, which means fewer places to mutate the genome. When you have a fixed number of constant nodes, the program will create new constants by combining the existing constants through operator nodes. Although we might not have 0.5, we can represent that value as 1 divided by 2.

4.5 Chapter Summary

The genetic algorithms that we saw in the last chapter required that their solutions be implemented as fixed-length arrays. In this chapter, we learned that trees also evolve as they implement the simple programs and mathemat-

4.5 Chapter Summary

ical expressions discussed in the previous sections. Specifically, tree-centric crossover and mutation operators evolved these trees.

Computer programs and mathematical expressions can be represented as trees. Each tree node is a function, and the branches under the tree specify the arguments to those functions. The recursive nature of these trees allows complex expressions to be encoded.

Crossover has the greatest chance of producing well-adapted children when both parents are relatively similar. Of course, nature has many examples of this idea. Even if the possibility existed that a humming bird and an elephant could mate and reproduce, their offspring would be ill suited for most every environment. In nature, offspring between species are very rare. Thus, imposing these same restrictions on evolutionary algorithms can be useful. Chapter 5, "Speciation," shows how to implement this constraint.

Chapter 5

Speciation

- Threshold Speciation
- Cluster Speciation
- Crossover and Mutation for Trees
- Fitting Equations

Speciation is the evolutionary process by which a new biological species arises. The biologist Orator F. Cook (1906) seems to have been the first to coin the term *speciation* for the splitting of lineages of organisms. Merriam-Webster (2014) defines a species as a "group of animals or plants that are similar and can produce young animals or plants: a group of related animals or plants that is smaller than a genus." For the purposes of nature-inspired algorithms, the key part of this definition is that members of a species can produce offspring.

If an evolutionary algorithm uses speciation, it limits crossover to members of the same species. Crossover can have a very high failure rate as it takes traits from two or more individuals and splices them together. This process works best when the parents are somewhat similar to each other. So far, the evolutionary algorithms presented in this book have created the possibility for any fit solutions to become parents together.

Consider how nature segregates organisms for reproduction. Only members of the same species produce offspring. Even if it were possible, the offspring of a humming bird and an elephant would probably not be a successful organism. Even if we found the best elephant and the best humming bird, their offspring would surely not be the best at anything. Fundamentally, speciation is an attempt to improve the probability of success for offspring produced by crossover.

5.1 Speciation Implementations

Not every nature-inspired algorithm utilizes speciation. However, the algorithms that do use speciation implement it in a similar manner. In every operation, the first issue to surface is the likeness of the genomes. Do they share characteristics of the same species? This question implies that a process exists to compare two genomes. In fact, there are several methods. However, comparing two fixed-length genomes from a genetic algorithm is quite different from analyzing two genomes from a tree-based genetic algorithm. Therefore, we will discuss genome comparison later in the chapter.

No matter how you compare two genomes, the result will be a floating-point number, which is the distance between the two genomes. A lower number indicates two genomes that are relatively similar. A higher number indicates two genomes that are more different.

You will learn two different ways to interpret this similarity measurement between two genomes. Additionally, you will see a variety of approaches to calculate it, beginning with threshold speciation.

5.1.1 Threshold Speciation

Threshold speciation is a very simple speciation algorithm that relies solely on the similarity measurement between two genomes. This speciation algorithm uses the following two training parameters: species count and the starting speciation threshold.

5.1 Speciation Implementations

The species count is the desired number of species. A common default setting for this parameter is 30. This means that the algorithm will try to hold the species count at 30. However, threshold speciation makes no guarantees that the species count will be held at this setting. Rather, the species threshold will be adjusted to move in the direction of this count.

The species threshold value specifies the minimum similarity measurement that two genomes must have to be the same species. This value is just the starting point because the threshold level is adjusted to maintain the desired species count. Next, the initial generation is divided into species. This division is called speciation.

An evolutionary algorithm begins by placing the first generated genome into its own species. The second genome will join the first genome if its similarity measurement is below the speciation similarity threshold. This process continues for the entire population. Once all population members have been processed, each genome should belong to a species. This process will repeat during each generation.

At the end of each generation, the algorithm considers the species count. If there are too many species, then the speciation threshold will increase. In other words, the genomes will need to be more similar in order to be grouped in the same species. This result will decrease the number of species. If there are not enough species, then the speciation threshold will decrease, which should increase the number of species. The balancing act continues for each generation. By adjusting the speciation threshold, the algorithm keeps the species count close to the level specified by the training parameter.

5.1.2 Clustering Speciation

I have found that threshold speciation increases the effectiveness of crossover operations in my algorithms. However, threshold speciation is not the only way to divide a population into species. Clustering is another speciation algorithm. At the time of this book's publication, I have not written any clustering speciation examples. I will likely add some examples in the future. In the meantime, this section will provide an overview of clustering so that you can utilize it in your own algorithms.

Clustering speciation uses a clustering algorithm, such as k-means or k-medoids to provide speciation. The advantage over threshold speciation is that clustering strictly enforces the desired species count. Typically, a clustering speciation algorithm will have only the species count training parameter, and the algorithm will exactly divide each generation of the population into that count of species. Genomes will fall into these species based on their similarity to each other. It is important to note that the members of a population will not necessarily split evenly into species. It is quite possible for one species to contain a handful of individuals and another to contain hundreds.

Clustering algorithms are a form of unsupervised learning. In other words, there are no right or wrong answers–the computer simply provides insights into the data. A clustering algorithm takes data and divides them into clusters. The data in each of these clusters have similar characteristics. Therefore, clustering algorithms are a natural choice for speciation because they excel at grouping things.

K-means can be an effective clustering algorithm. In fact, the first volume of the *AI for Humans* series features an example on how to implement the K-means algorithm. This book, though, deals with how to utilize k-means for speciation. K-means works best for speciating fixed-length arrays because it cannot operate with only the genome similarity measurement, unlike threshold speciation. K-means speciation must be able to create a centroid for each species.

The centroid of a species is the stereotypical representation of its members. In other words, it is the average species member. However, the centroid does not actually exist as a genome because it is essentially a concept. For example, *Time* (2011) published an article called *The World's Most Typical Person is a 28-Year-Old Chinese Man* that illustrates this idea.

http://newsfeed.time.com/2011/03/04/just-8-999-999-like-him/

In the article, a 28-year-old Chinese man is essentially a centroid for the entire human race. His face is computer rendered, and he does not exist. He simply represents the averaging of every existing feature from human genomes.

You can apply this same principle to artificial genomes. For fixed-length arrays, the centroid is simply the average of each array element across the genomes in the species. Nevertheless, these centroids are the primary drawback to k-means speciation, especially compared to threshold speciation.

Reliance on a centroid is a problem because centroids may not always be available. Even though calculating a centroid for a fixed-length array is relatively easy, it's not always possible to calculate for a genome represented as a tree, as we saw in Chapter 4. As a result, genetic programming cannot utilize k-means speciation; k-medoids algorithms are preferable for genetic programming.

The k-medoids algorithm, introduced by Kaufman (1987), works similarly to the k-means algorithm except that it does not require a centroid. In other words, that k-medoids can perform speciation on a population using only the genome similarity measurement discussed earlier in this chapter. It functions by choosing a genome calculated to be the most representative of the species to replace the centroid. Therefore, the population is broken into the correct number of clusters, or species.

5.2 Speciation in Genetic Algorithms

Now you will learn to calculate the similarity measure for genomes for both genetic algorithms and genetic programming. In genetic algorithms, you can apply regular distance calculations to compare the similarity between two genomes. To perform speciation with a genetic algorithm, Euclidean distance is a good choice. Simply calculate Euclidean distance as the genome similarity measurement. Consider the following two genomes expressed as fixed-length arrays:

```
Genome 1: [2.0, 3.0, 5.0]
Genome 2: [1.0, 2.0, 1.0]
```

The following equation calculates the Euclidean distance:

$$\sqrt{(2-1)^2 + (3-2)^2 + (5-1)^2} = 4.242641 \qquad (5.1)$$

The distance shows the similarities between the two genomes. If 4.252641 were below the speciation threshold, these two genomes would be in the same species.

5.3 Speciation in Genetic Programming

Calculating the similarity measure for trees in genetic programming is only slightly more complex than genetic algorithms. Because I have not found many published methods for comparing genetic programming trees, my method is to traverse the tree and keep a count of the number of nodes that are the same type. To see this method, consider Figure 5.1.

Figure 5.1: Comparing Trees

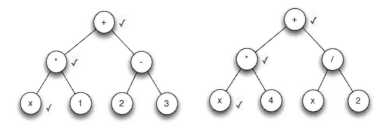

Looking at the above trees, you can see that they are somewhat different. Only three nodes match. Because there are 7 nodes in the entire tree, the similarity is only 3/7, or 42% the same. The exact calculation is summarized in Equation 5.1.

$$\frac{\Delta_{t1,t2}}{max(N_{t1}, N_{t2})} \tag{5.2}$$

As you can see from the above equation, we divide the number of changed nodes between the two trees (*t1* & *t2*) and then divide by the total node count of the largest tree.

5.4 Using Speciation

The structure of an evolutionary algorithm is changed by the addition of speciation. To implement speciation, sum the scores of each species to produce a total population score. Assign each species a percentage of this total score based on how large that species score is relative to the entire population. This percentage determines how much of the next generation will come from offspring of that species.

For example, consider a population of 1,000 genomes and 10 species. Species #1 has a total score of 1,000, and the total population score is 15,000. Species #1 has 1,000/15,000 (7%) of the total score. In short, species #1 will produce 7% of the 1,000 genomes in the next population. To produce these 70 genomes, regular selection is performed inside of the species to determine the new parents.

Now you will observe the training for the iris data set using threshold speciation. This process uses a genetic algorithm to initiate the exact same training that was performed in Chapter 4. Adding speciation allows the training to complete in 250 generations. The training progress follows:

```
Iteration #1, Score=0.17495982354737508, Species Count: 937
Iteration #2, Score=0.1706156692994128, Species Count: 829
Iteration #3, Score=0.1706156692994128, Species Count: 697
Iteration #4, Score=0.1706156692994128, Species Count: 358
Iteration #5, Score=0.16155391035729205, Species Count: 159
Iteration #6, Score=0.1590871219942837, Species Count: 159
Iteration #7, Score=0.1590871219942837, Species Count: 111
Iteration #8, Score=0.1590871219942837, Species Count: 98
Iteration #9, Score=0.1590871219942837, Species Count: 54
Iteration #10, Score=0.1590871219942837, Species Count: 52
Iteration #11, Score=0.15729238266187578, Species Count: 24
Iteration #12, Score=0.15729238266187578, Species Count: 23
...
Iteration #249, Score=0.052048101781812586, Species Count: 600
Iteration #250, Score=0.049240602469552884, Species Count: 828
Final score: 0.049240602469552884
...
```

As you can see from the above output, the species count is initially very high because the randomly generated genomes have little in common with each other. After several generations, the genomes become specialized, and the species count quickly drops. Additionally, the speciation algorithm is lowering the speciation threshold in an effort to obtain the 30 species count that I requested for the above run. Near the end of the algorithm's run, the species count usually increases greatly as the genomes converge to common solutions.

5.5 Chapter Summary

Speciation is a method for improving the probability that genetic crossover produces successful offspring. In nature, only organisms of the same species produce offspring. As in nature, crossover tends to produce better offspring from similar parent genomes. Evolutionary algorithms can increase the effectiveness of their crossover by employing speciation.

To implement speciation, you must have a way to compare the similarity of two genomes. Comparison methods will vary according to the different genome types. For fixed-length genetic algorithm genomes, you can utilize Euclidean distance. For genetic programming trees, you can use tree comparison.

Chapters 3 and 4 focused primarily on competitive algorithms. The next two chapters will examine cooperative algorithms. As you will discover, comparative and cooperative algorithms have many differences. In Chapter 6, we will start with particle swarm optimization.

5.5 Chapter Summary

Chapter 6

Particle Swarm Optimization

- Cooperative Populations
- Flocking, Swarming, and Schooling
- Particle Swarm Optimization

Thus far, implementing competitive populations has been the primary interest of this book. Now, the focus will shift to cooperative populations in Chapters 6 and 7. Both types of populations will work together to find optimal solutions.

The competitive populations in the previous chapters improved by creating successively better generations of solutions. Unlike competitive populations, cooperative populations will not progress through successive generations. A fixed set of individuals will improve its solutions as the iterations progress. In other words, rather than adjusting the genetic code, as we did in competitive algorithms, each of the cooperating individuals adjusts its position.

6.1 Flocking

Flocks of birds in the sky illustrate the idea of cooperative behavior. While flocking may appear as a very complex behavior, many different animals exhibit it. Indeed, expressions like "flock of birds," "swarm of insects," "school of fish," and "herd of cows" reveal the identical behavior of grouping through the various names for it.

Craig Reynolds (1986) first replicated flocking behavior on a computer with his simulation program, Boids. To all appearances, a flocking algorithm may seem complex; a programmer would probably create an object to handle all the individuals in the flock.

Additionally, the programmer would need to develop routines to determine the direction of the flock. Other criteria for the program include whether a flock should be split into two or more, the size of a flock, and the process by which new members are admitted. As a result, this type of program could become very complex. Figure 6.1 is a flocking simulation.

Figure 6.1: Flocking Simulation

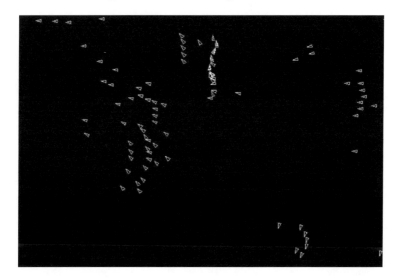

6.1 Flocking

Despite these concerns, the programmer still needs to ask the following question: Is it really necessary for the flocking program to be complex? Nature answers this question with a resounding no. Its apparent complexity stems from very simple rules. Consequently, nature can inspire us to create a straightforward process to simulate a flock of birds. The algorithm that produced Figure 6.1 is actually very simple; it has only three rules.

- **Separation** - Avoid crowding neighbors (short-range repulsion).
- **Alignment** - Steer towards average heading of neighbors.
- **Cohesion** - Steer towards average position of neighbors (long-range attraction).

These three rules are the only requirement for flocking. The bird example demonstrates the utter simplicity in seemingly complex behavior. The particles, or birds, all move at a constant speed. Each particle also has an angle that defines its direction. Furthermore, the particles cannot accelerate or slow down. They can only turn.

Flocking rules also establish an ideal angle for the particle's direction. In other words, the rules specify the angle that a particle would like to be heading. Since a particle cannot immediately jump to the ideal angle, it will begin to turn in that direction. This behavior is consistent with real life. If a bird is heading south and wants to change directions to go north, the bird must take some amount of time to turn to the new heading. A specific percent regulates the particle's desire to follow the rules.

You can experiment with these three parameters to see their effect. It's important to realize that many combinations will not produce flocking behavior at all. However, the following default values work well:

- **Separation**: 0.25
- **Alignment**: 0.5
- **Cohesion**: 0.01

To observe the effect of one rule in isolation, set that rule to 1.0 and the others to 0.0. For example, segregating cohesion will cause all of the particles to converge on a few locations in the universe. No randomness will occur in this universe at all unless you place the particles in random locations at the outset. Beyond this placement, the program will no longer generate random numbers. You can practice with an online example at the following URL:

http://www.heatonresearch.com/fun/flock

Flocking is a fascinating topic because it shows how a universe, such as the above program, can exhibit seemingly complex behavior. Consider our universe; it appears very complex. Fields of study such as physics, chemistry, biology, and others attempt to develop models to explain natural phenomena. Scientists seek a theory of everything to unify all physical laws into a simple set of underlying laws (Weinberg, 1993). However, no one has made a unifying discovery. The best we have now is a theory of almost everything, or the fundamental forces theory (Oerter, 2006).

The fundamental forces theory categorizes many physical interactions in terms of four central forces governed by the following universal constants:

- Strong: 1
- Electromagnetic: 1/137
- Weak: 10^{-6}
- Gravity: $6 * 10^{-39}$

If you would like to read more about the fundamental forces theory, the following URL provides a good overview:

http://hyperphysics.phy-astr.gsu.edu/hbase/forces/funfor.html

The four constants play a role in the real universe that is similar to the separation, alignment, and cohesion constants in the flocking universe. These constants define how their respective universes function. Of course, the real universe is not deterministic, or entirely predictable, as stated in Bell's theorem (1966). On the contrary, the flocking algorithm absolutely defines how a particle behaves. Actual physical laws give probabilities of how a particle might behave.

6.2 Particle Swarm Optimization

Programmers can also utilize flocking as a search algorithm, allowing it to optimize the parameters of a model. In this way, it can train neural networks, Bayesian networks, support vector machines, and other machine learning algorithms. This type of algorithm is particle swarm optimization. In 1995, Kennedy and Eberhart introduced the PSO algorithm. Unlike many learning algorithms, no math beyond basic arithmetic is required. Thus, PSO is relatively easy to understand.

First, you must comprehend its mapping strategy to a search space. Consider a lone particle in a one-dimensional search space. This particle can only move left or right. In a two-dimensional search space, it can move in two dimensions, like in a checkerboard. A three-dimensional particle can move in three dimensions. Our world is three-dimensional. Consequently, a bird can fly up or down, left or right, forwards or backwards.

Unlike in nature, PSO can operate in very high dimension spaces. The ability to search in higher dimensions is advantageous because most problems have more than three dimensions. Each parameter in the model is a dimension. Fundamentally, the parameters of a model reduce to an array of floating-point numbers.

In a neural network, once you specify the number of neurons and the way that they fit into layers, the number of weights in this network does not change. As training progresses, these weights are changed to cause the neural network to produce the correct output for a given input. These weights become the dimensions for a PSO search. You can think of the neural network as flying through these dimensions, looking for an optimal position that is the set of weights that most closely map the inputs to the desired output.

6.2.1 Particles

PSO uses a fixed population of particles. Often this number is 30; however, the algorithm can handle larger or smaller values. Each particle holds several values. These values are summarized here.

- Current position (or model parameters)
- Best position & score
- Velocity Vector

The current and best positions are vectors of equal length compared to the model's parameter-vector length. Additionally, the algorithm keeps a current score for both the current and best positions. Keeping a particle's best position allows the particle to explore space away from its best position. The ultimate solution provided by the PSO algorithm will be the particle with the most desirable best score. Depending on the goal of the PSO, whether it is maximization or minimization, a desirable score might be high or low.

Particles are never at rest; they constantly move. Velocity is speed and direction. The velocity vector is the same length as the model. One can express the velocity of a real-world object as the speed at which the object is moving in each of the three dimensions. Likewise, the particle has a velocity component for each of the dimensions, which can be negative or positive, specifying the direction of the particle. Unlike the flocking particles in the last section, all PSO particles do not move at the same speed. They will accelerate and decelerate as they move about the search space.

In these movements, the particles will look for the model parameters, or coordinates, that provide the best score. The velocities furnish the direction and speed of the particles, which are added to the current coordinate, or weights. For example, if the third dimension were currently 10, and the velocity were -0.5, then the third dimension would move to 9.5. As the particles move around, the best solution for the entire system is the particle with the lowest best error.

6.2 Particle Swarm Optimization

The velocities are initially set to random values. However, they do not stay at these random values. The real power of the PSO algorithm is the way that these velocities are updated. This indicates that learning occurs as the score increases.

6.2.2 Velocity Calculation

The iteration updates the velocity components, or dimensions, completely independently of each other. Equation 6.1 shows how this update occurs.

```
v[] = v[] + c1 * uniform_random() * (pbest[] - param[]) + c2 *
    uniform_random() * (gbest[] - param[])
```

It happens in such a way that the particle will steer towards the particle's best vector (**pbest**) and the global best vector (**gbest**). The movement to the particle's best is scaled by **c1**, and the movement towards global best is scaled by **c2**, allowing each particle to divide its search between the global (**c2**) and local (**c1**) best.

These values are summarized as follows:

- **v[]** - The current velocity. Each array position is assigned a new value in the above equation.

- **param[]** - The parameters, or coordinates, that correspond to the velocity of the same array index.

- **pbest[]** - The best parameter array found by this particle.

- **gbest[]** - The best parameter array found by any of the particles.

- **c1** - The learning rate for the particle to converge to its own best. (Typically set to 2.)

- **c2** - The learning rate for the particle to converge to the overall best particle. (Typically set to 2.)

- **random_uniform()** - A random number between 0 and 1.

The only two parameters that must be set are two learning rates, specified by **c1** and **c2**. These values are typically both set to 2. Setting them to other values will affect performance of training. Experimentation will determine whether the setting improves or harms performance.

6.2.3 Implementation

It is not difficult to implement PSO in computer code. Listing 6.1 shows pseudocode that implements PSO.

Listing 6.1: Particle Swarm Optimization (PSO)

```
for i from 1 to particle_count:
  particle = new Particle()
  particles.add(particle)
  # Randomize particle initial state
  for j from 0 to param_count-1:
    # Set particle velocities to random
    particle.v[j] = random_uniform(0,1)
    # Set particle velocities to random
    particle.param[j] = random_uniform(0,1)
    # Set particle best to match the weights
    particle.pbest[j] = particle.param[j]

best_score = min_float
# Main loop
while best_score<required_score:
  for each particle in particles:
    score = score_function(particle)
    # Update the best particle best
    if score > particle.best_score:
      particle.best_score = score
      particle.pbest = particle.param.clone()
```

6.2 Particle Swarm Optimization

```
    # Update global best
    if score>best_score:
      best_score = score
      gbest = particle.param.clone()
  # Move the particles
  for each p in particles:
    for j from 0 to param_count-1:
      p.v[j] = p.v[j] +
        c1 * random_uniform() * (p.pbest[j] - p.param[j])
        + c2 * random_uniform() * (gbest[j] - p.parms[j])
      p.param[j] = p.param[j] + p.v[j]
```

The above code begins by creating a number of particles equal to **particle_count**. These particles are stored in a collection named **particles**. Each particle is given a random velocity and parameters (coordinates). Each particle's **pbest** collection is initially set to the same value as that particle's initial random position because that is the only location the particle has seen.

Because we seek to maximize the score variable, the **best_score** variable is initialized to the minimum possible value for a floating-point number. This terrible score ensures that the main loop will update the best score to the current score on the main loop's first pass.

The main loop begins by calculating the current score of a particle. If the particle has reached a new personal best, then we must update **pbest** with this new score. Furthermore, if this score is better than the current global **best_score,** then we update both the **best_score** variable and **gbest** vector. The **gbest** vector always holds the best parameters encountered so far. The main loop begins by updating the velocity vector.

PSO optimization can be applied to the RBF neural network model. PSO trains an RBF neural network by adjusting its model parameters. This method was used in Chapter 3, "Genetic Algorithms," for RBF. In that chapter, the genetic algorithm adjusted the model parameters to achieve a better model fit. Most training algorithms work this way. The only difference between PSO and a genetic algorithm is the adjustment of the model parameters. You can see the results of using PSO to fit an RBF neural network model to the iris data set in the following example:

```
Iteration #1, Score=0.2608812647245383,
Iteration #2, Score=0.2608812647245383,
```

```
Iteration #3,  Score=0.2608812647245383,
Iteration #4,  Score=0.2608812647245383,
Iteration #5,  Score=0.20548629451773479,
Iteration #6,  Score=0.20548629451773479,
Iteration #7,  Score=0.1456525667121654,
Iteration #8,  Score=0.1456525667121654,
Iteration #9,  Score=0.1456525667121654,
Iteration #10, Score=0.1456525667121654,
...
Iteration #56, Score=0.0517051622593003,
Iteration #57, Score=0.0517051622593003,
Iteration #58, Score=0.0517051622593003,
Iteration #59, Score=0.045664739474608994,
Final score: 0.045664739474608994
[-0.55, 0.24, -0.86, -0.91] -> Iris-setosa, Ideal: Iris-setosa
[-0.66, -0.16, -0.86, -0.91] -> Iris-setosa, Ideal: Iris-setosa
...
[0.22, -0.16, 0.42, 0.58] -> Iris-virginica, Ideal: Iris-virginica
[0.05,  0.16, 0.49, 0.83] -> Iris-virginica, Ideal: Iris-virginica
[-0.11, -0.16, 0.38, 0.41] -> Iris-virginica, Ideal: Iris-
    virginica
```

PSO is an efficient means of training an RBF neural network. In this case, only 59 training iterations were required.

6.3 Chapter Summary

Chapter 6 introduced flocking and particle swarm optimization. Both algorithms use particles. Flocking utilizes individual particles to simulate flocks of birds. Three simple rules govern the seemingly complex flocking behavior.

Particle swarm optimization (PSO) extends the flocking behavior to become an optimization algorithm. PSO can optimize a vector of parameters to achieve a desirable score, which allows an optimal RBF neural network model to fit a data set such as the iris data set. PSO permits the particles to fly through potentially high-dimensional space looking for optimal solutions.

PSO is not the only cooperative population that I will present. Chapter 7 introduces ant colony optimization (ACO). This nature-inspired algorithm uses individual ants searching for optimal paths to food, and it is based on the pheromone trails that ants leave behind to guide others from their colony.

Chapter 7

Ant Colony Optimization

- Ant Colony Optimization (ACO)
- Discrete ACO
- Continuous ACO

Ant colony optimization (ACO) is another algorithm inspired by nature. Unlike particle swarm optimization (PSO), ACO is applicable to both continuous and discrete problems. As a result, ACO is interchangeable with a genetic algorithm (GA). The continuous and discrete versions of ACO differ considerably, as this chapter will show. Marco Dorigo (1992) introduced discrete ACO in his PhD thesis. Based on this research, Christian Blum and Krzysztof Socha (2005) published a continuous version of ACO.

The foraging behavior of ants influences both the discrete and continuous versions of ACO. In nature, ants initially wander randomly in their search for food. Upon finding food, the ant returns to the colony while laying down pheromone trails. The presence of pheromone increases the probability that an ant will move into that location and continue on that trail. If other ants discover these paths, a strong probability exists that they will not continue traveling at random. Instead, they will find the trail, returning and reinforcing it in their search for food. However, ants will still occasionally travel at random and possibly find shorter paths.

Over time, the pheromone trail evaporates, reducing its attractive strength. Therefore, as an ant spends more time traveling down the path and back again, there is less time for the pheromones to evaporate. Consequently, ants march more frequently over a short path, causing the pheromone density to become higher on shorter paths compared to longer ones. Additionally, pheromone evaporation encourages exploration beyond the initial paths. Without evaporation, the favorite paths of the first ants tend to be extremely attractive to later ants (Holldobler, 1990). Figure 7.1 shows ants foraging for food with the majority of the ants following the established path.

Figure 7.1: Ants Foraging

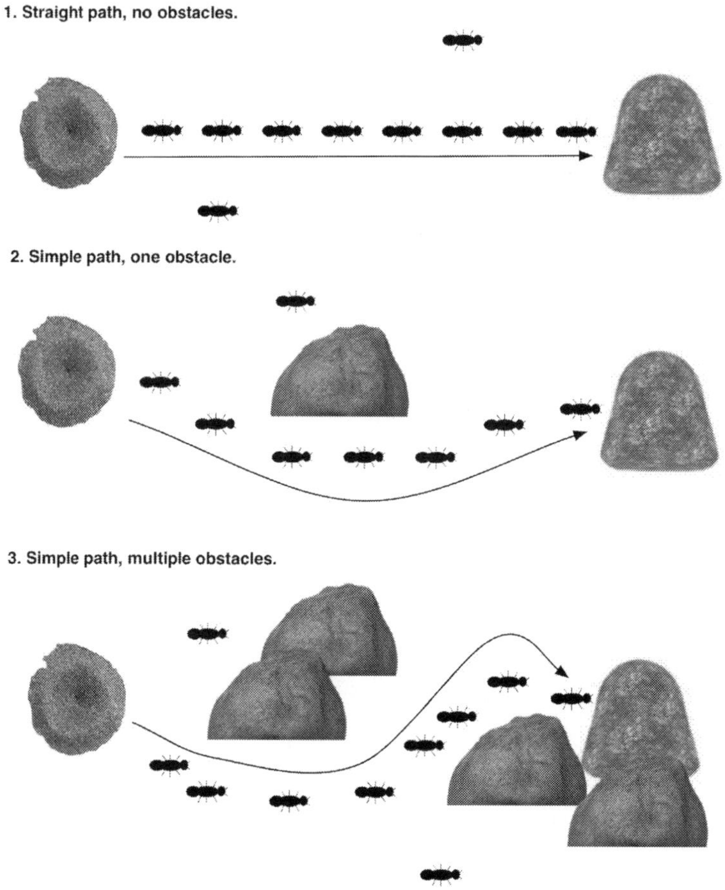

1. Straight path, no obstacles.

2. Simple path, one obstacle.

3. Simple path, multiple obstacles.

Thus, when one ant finds a shorter path from the colony to a food source, other ants are more likely to follow that path. This positive feedback eventually leads to most of the ants following a single path. Some ants will still forage randomly to find shorter paths. The ACO algorithm mimics this behavior with simulated ants marching around a solution graph that represents the problem to solve.

7.1 Discrete Ant Colony Optimization

Similar to other algorithms, ACO employs different approaches for continuous and discrete learning. Continuous learning deals with calculating numeric values, whereas discrete learning deals with recognizing non-numeric values. In this section, I will show you the discrete form of the ACO.

The traveling salesman problem (TSP) is a great example of a discrete problem. Most discrete problems involve finding the optimal arrangement of a collection of items. Each arrangement must be scored. The ACO can be designed to either minimize or maximize this score. The typical definition of the TSP involves the arrangement of cities that provide the shortest path through the cities without revisiting any city twice.

The following output shows ACO to find a solution to the TSP:

```
Iteration: 1, Best Path Length = 1696.0
Iteration: 2, Best Path Length = 1571.0
Iteration: 3, Best Path Length = 1524.0
Iteration: 4, Best Path Length = 1454.0
Iteration: 5, Best Path Length = 1454.0
Iteration: 6, Best Path Length = 1454.0
Iteration: 7, Best Path Length = 1454.0
Iteration: 8, Best Path Length = 1454.0
Iteration: 9, Best Path Length = 1454.0
Iteration: 10, Best Path Length = 1454.0
...
Iteration: 98, Best Path Length = 1403.0
Iteration: 99, Best Path Length = 1403.0
Iteration: 100, Best Path Length = 1403.0
Iteration: 101, Best Path Length = 1403.0
Iteration: 102, Best Path Length = 1403.0
Iteration: 103, Best Path Length = 1403.0
```

```
Good solution found:
18>11>24>7>31>32>46>44>8>21>15>36>37>6>2>12>5>43>40>17>23>4>
14>20>0>38>33>10>49>45>29>9>28>48>19>3>34>30>27>1>35>26>25>
22>16>13>47>42>41>39
```

The above example sought to minimize the path through the cities. At iteration 103, the example had converged on a solution with a length of 1403.

The implementation of discrete ACO defines several constants and starting values listed here.

- **ant_count** - It's the number of ants in the algorithm. The default is 30.
- **alpha** - This constant specifies the attractiveness of the pheromone trail. The default is 1.
- **beta** - This constant sets the attractiveness of better state transitions (from one node to another). The default is 5.
- **evaporation** - This constant determines how quickly the pheromone path evaporates. The default is 0.5.
- **q** - This constant controls the amount of pheromone that the nodes of a path share for a trip. The default is 500.
- **initial_pheromone** - This term is the initial value of the pheromone trails. The default is 1.0.
- **pr** - This constant defines the probability that an ant will simply wander to any cell. The default is 0.01.

These training settings control the algorithm. Adjusting them may help the ACO algorithm to find an acceptable solution faster. However, you need to follow some general guidelines for adjusting the training parameters. Increasing the **evaporation** setting will cause the algorithm to try new solutions over refining the current solution. For larger search areas, increasing the **q** and **ant_count** may be necessary. Increasing **beta** makes the algorithm greedier and less willing to experiment with path segments containing worse scores. Increasing **alpha** makes the algorithm more inclined to follow established trails rather than experiment to find new trails.

7.1 Discrete Ant Colony Optimization

7.1.1 ACO Initialization

Discrete ACO typically finds an optimal ordering of items in a list. These items are usually visualized as a graph and have one continuous line connecting them. Each item must be visited once, and the same one is never visited twice. In graph terminology, each item visited is called a node, and the line segments between nodes are called an edge.

The first step for the ACO algorithm is to initialize the pheromone trails and ant parameters. A square grid stores the pheromone trails through the nodes. The square grid's width is equal to the number of nodes to visit. This grid represents the pheromone strength between any node and the other nodes. Since we do not track pheromone strength between a node and itself, we do not use the diagonal of this grid. We initialize the grid to the **initial_pheromone** training setting. Figure 7.2 shows an initialized grid for three nodes.

Figure 7.2: Initialized Grid for Three Nodes

		To		
		n1	n2	n3
From	n1		n1->n2	n1->n3
	n2	n2->n1		n2->n3
	n3	n3->n1	n3->n2	

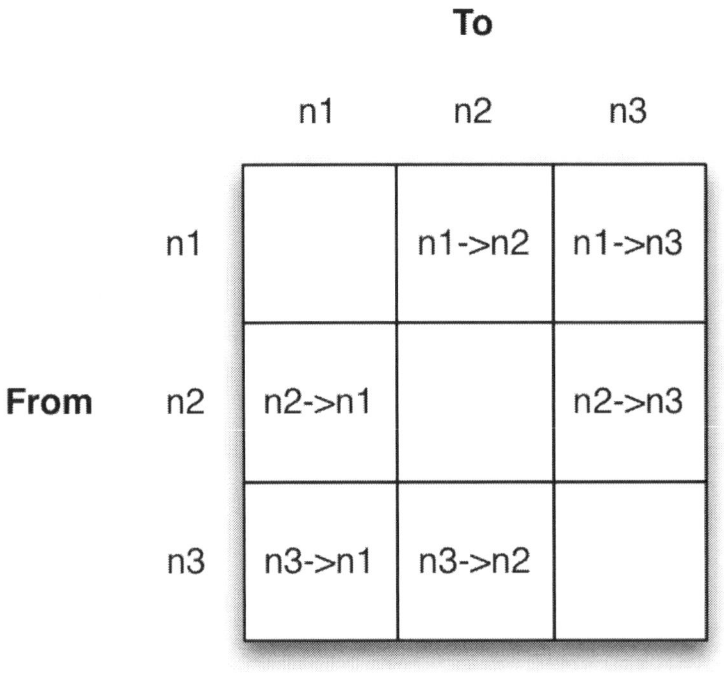

Each ant must also maintain a list of the nodes that it has visited, which allows the ant to return to the colony after meeting its objective. For a discrete ACO algorithm, the goal will either be to visit every node or to visit one or more specific nodes.

The classic traveling salesman problem exemplifies the goal of visiting every node, as explained in an earlier chapter. Once the ant has visited every node, it will return and reinforce a pheromone trail, creating a path. You can adapt this goal to many problems beyond the TSP. Finding the shortest path while visiting all nodes on a graph is a common computer science problem. Many brute-force and machine learning algorithms are devoted to this problem.

The goal of visiting a specific node is analogous to ants finding a food source in nature. The goal node is the one that contains a food source for the ants. However, they do not care about visiting each node. If the goal is to visit a specific node, the ants concern themselves with the shortest path to that food source. This algorithm has many real world applications. For example, you could use an ACO to find the most efficient highway route between St. Louis and Los Angeles.

7.1.2 Ant Movement

The first step requires the ant to move forward to the next cell. If it is the first cell that the ant will visit, then a random cell is simply chosen. The ant can choose any of the nodes as the starting step. Sometimes, the ant will also visit a random, non-visited square with a probability equal to **pr**.

If the ant is not taking its first step, and we have not chosen to select a random move, then we must compute a probability for all non-visited nodes that the ant selects. Equation 7.1 computes this selection.

$$p_{xy}^k = \frac{(\tau_{xy}^\alpha)(\eta_{xy}^\beta)}{\sum_{y \in \text{allowed}_y}(\tau_{xy}^\alpha)(\eta_{xy}^\beta)} \tag{7.1}$$

This equation calculates the probability of moving from node x to node y at iteration k. Looking at the numerator, we have pheromone deposited between x and y given by *tau*. We raise *tau* to the power of *alpha*, as the training

7.1 Discrete Ant Colony Optimization

parameter *alpha* governs the effectiveness of pheromones. In the numerator, we also have *eta*, which represents the value of moving from node x to node y. We raise *eta* to the power of *beta*, as the training parameter *beta* governs the influence of cost on the ant movement. We divide the product of *eta* and *beta* for the desired x and y by the summation of the *tau* and *eta* for all allowed node transitions.

The summation in the denominator of Equation 7.1 looks at the total value of the entire unvisited graph from the desirability of score and pheromone. We subsequently evaluate each potential move as the percentage of that total value to determine the probability of each potential move being chosen. Based on these probabilities, a random selection is made to decide the next cell for the given ant.

The use of Equation 7.1 requires several pages of code. The probability calculation is shown in Listing 7.1.

Listing 7.1: Ant Movement Probability

```
# Calculate probabilities
sub calculate_probability(index, ant):
  # We will return an array with the probability of
  # each node.
  result = new[length(graph)]

  # Choose the node that the ant just visited.
  # This should never be called before the ant visits
  # the first node.
  i = ant.path[length(path)-1]

  # Calculate the denominator the path probabilities.
  d = 0
  for l from 0 to length(graph)-1:
    # Do not count visited nodes
    if not ant.visited(l):
      # Sum the pheromone and score values
      d = d + (pheromone[i][l] ^ alpha) * (graph.score(i,l)^beta)

  # Now calculate the individual probabilities.
  for j from 0 to length(graph)-1:
    if ant.visited(j):
      # Zero probability if already visited
      result[j] = 0.0
```

```
    else:
      # Calculate probability numerator.
      n = (pheromone[i][j]^alpha) * (1.0/graph.score(i,j)^alpha)
      result[j] = n/d

  # Return the probability vector
  return result
```

The above function is given the current path index and the ant. This function will return a vector of probabilities for the ant moving from its current path index (current position) to any of other nodes. The ant has zero probability of moving to its own node or a visited node. Equation 7.1 is fully implemented in Listing 7.1. The external function **graph.score** is called to determine the score/cost in moving between two nodes. Because the implementation of pseudocode depends on the problem to resolve, I do not provide pseudocode for the score function. The examples of this book's code do contain a score function for the TSP as well as score functions for other examples that might have been added since publication.

Listing 7.2 performs the selection of the ant's next step.

Listing 7.2: Choose the Ant's Next Step

```
# Choose the next step for an ant.
sub choose_next_step(ant):
  # If this is the first step then just choose a
  # random (non-selected) node.
  # Otherwise choose a random (non-selected) node with
  # pr probability.
  if length(ant.path) == 0 or uniform_random()<pr:
    index = -1
    # Choose a random(non-visited) node
    while index==-1 or not ant.visited(index):
      index = uniform_random(0,length(graph)-1)
  else:
    # Obtain an array of the probabilities of this ant
    # moving to all other nodes.
    prob = calculate_probability(index,ant)

    # Obtain a random number between 0 and 1 that determines
    # the chosen node.
    r = uniform_random()
    sum = 0
```

7.1 Discrete Ant Colony Optimization

```
# We will loop forward adding each probability to sum.
# Once we pass r, we have selected a node, with the
# correct probability.
for in from 0 to length(graph)-1:
  sum = sum + prob[i]
  if sum>r:
    return i

# Should not happen, but most programming languages require a
# return value. If we did get here, then r was assigned to
# something beyond 1.0, or the probabilities added to
# more than 1.0.
return -1
```

The above function calls **calculate_probability** from Listing 7.1 and receives a list of probabilities for every node that the ant has not yet visited. If the ant has not yet taken its first step, then we do not calculate probabilities. For the ant's first step, we simply choose a random node. To encourage exploration beyond the pheromone trails, we also pick a random node with **pr** probability.

The last two listings deal with the preliminaries of probability calculation. With these preliminaries complete, we can march the ants forward through all the required steps. Listing 7.3 shows this process.

Listing 7.3: March the Ants

```
# March all ants for one iteration.
sub march():
  # Select each node, up to the max number of nodes (the length of
    the graph).
  # For example, if there are 10 cities in the TSP, loop from 1 to
    10.
  for i from 1 to length(graph):
    # Loop over all ants.
    for each ant in ants:
      # Choose the ant's next step
      next = choose_next_step(ant)
      # Record ant's next step
      ant.path.add(next)
```

The **march** function is executed once per iteration. It will cause the ants to march through all required nodes, which will mean visiting each city for the TSP. The **march** function calls the **choose_next_step** function and then records the chosen step.

7.1.3 Pheromone Update

Once the ants have all marched through their complete paths, the pheromone trails must be updated. This two-part process considers both evaporation and pheromones deposited by the ants. Equation 7.2 summarizes this update.

$$\tau_{xy} = \rho \tau_{xy} + \sum_k \Delta \tau_{xy}^k \tag{7.2}$$

The variable *tau* represents the pheromone strength between nodes x and y. We're calculating this value. The variable *rho* specifies the evaporation rate training argument. *Delta tau* represents the amount of pheromone left by an ant between x and y by ant k.

For the TSP, Equation 7.3 typically calculates *delta tau*. Problems other than TSP will likely use similar approaches.

$$\Delta \tau_{xy}^k = \begin{cases} Q/L_k & \text{if ant } k \text{ uses path segment } xy \text{ in its tour} \\ 0 & \text{otherwise} \end{cases} \tag{7.3}$$

It is important to note that the exponent k in Equation 7.3 indicates ant k; it does not signify to raise to the power of k. First, the algorithm performs the pheromone update. Next, you apply evaporation to all pheromone values. Listing 7.4 shows the implementation of the evaporation process.

7.1 Discrete Ant Colony Optimization

Listing 7.4: Pheromone Evaporation

```
# Loop over every row.
for row from 0 to length(pheromone)-1:
  # Loop over every column.
  for col from 0 to length(pheromone[row])-1:
    pheromone[row][col] = pheromone[row][col] * evaporation
```

The above code loops over every pheromone edge in the graph and multiplies it by the **evaporation** ratio. The default evaporation is 0.5, decreasing a 1.0-pheromone level to 0.5 on the first iteration. The second iteration would also reduce by half the pheromone level to 0.25. Once a location's pheromone level is reasonably close to zero, that location can be set to zero.

Next, we must update the pheromone trails that the ants created. This update is demonstrated in Listing 7.5.

Listing 7.5: Pheromone Update

```
# Loop over each ant
for each ant in ants:
  # Calculate the delta as the total pheromones (q) divided by
  # the score that the ant achieved.
  d = q / graph.score(ant)
  # Update the pheromones between all steps.  Subtract 2 to
  # calculate up to the 2nd to the last node (the last node
  # has no edge to any further nodes)
  for i from 0 to length(graph)-2:
    pheromone[ant.path[i]][i+1] = pheromone[ant.path[i]][i+1] + d
  # Update the final node's pheromone.
  pheromone[ant.path[len(ant.path)-1]][ant.path[0]] =
    pheromone[ant.path[len(ant.path)-1]][ant.path[0]] + d
```

The above code loops over every ant and applies Equation 7.3.

7.2 Continuous Ant Colony Optimization

The continuous version of ACO is based much more loosely on the pheromone trail paradigm of ants in nature. The continuous form of ACO is the most efficient algorithm for model fitting for the data sets presented in this book. ACO will typically adjust the RBF model's parameters to minimize a data set's error with less iteration than particle swarm optimization (PSO) and genetic algorithms (GA).

Like discrete ACO, the ants in a continuous ACO algorithm are candidate solutions. Each ant is a vector of floating-point parameters. If you are using the continuous ACO to fit a model, such as the RBF neural network, this vector specifies the weights and RBF parameters of the model. This vector of parameters is analogous to the position of the ant.

Unlike the discrete version of ACO, we do not view each element of the vector as a step in the path of the ant. With continuous ACO, each element is part of a high-dimensional position of the ant. The iteration moves each ant to a random position generated by a probability density function (PDF). This process is called sampling.

Random numbers sampled from a PDF are biased. The Gaussian, or normal distribution, is the PDF most commonly used for continuous ACO. The equation for a Gaussian PDF is shown in Equation 7.4.

$$g(x, \mu, \sigma) = \frac{1}{\sigma\sqrt{2\pi}} e^{-\frac{(x-\mu)^2}{2\sigma^2}} \qquad (7.4)$$

The above equation allows you to define the center and width of a PDF. The constant *mu* defines the center, or mean. The constant *sigma* defines the width, or standard deviation. Figure 7.3 shows the Gaussian PDF with several different *mu* and *sigma* values.

7.2 Continuous Ant Colony Optimization

Figure 7.3: Gaussian PDF's

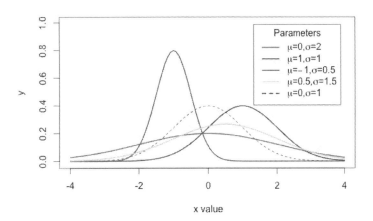

In the graph, the x-axis shows the value, and the y-axis shows the probability of selection. The random numbers sampled from each of the Gaussian have the greatest likelihood of being near the mean (or *mu*). The smaller the standard deviation (or *sigma*), the greater the likelihood that the random sample will fall very close to the mean.

The Gaussian PDF has a disadvantage because the variation in the shape of the Gaussian function is limited. A programmer cannot use a single Gaussian function to define a situation where there are two disjoint peaks, which are promising (Socha, 2007). A standard Gaussian function has only a single peak. To overcome this disadvantage, we will utilize a Gaussian kernel composed of several Gaussian functions. These kernels combine several Gaussian functions to express patterns more complex than the single-peaked shape of a Gaussian function. Equation 7.5 shows a Gaussian kernel.

$$G(x) = \sum_{l=1}^{k} \omega_l g(x, \mu_l, \sigma_l) \qquad (7.5)$$

As you can see, Equation 7.5 builds upon Equation 7.4 because we are now summing k Gaussian functions together. Each of these Gaussian functions has their own *mu* and *sigma* values. More importantly, a separate *omega* value weights each component Gaussian function. Based on its fitness, you will adjust the *omega* value for each Gaussian function. Figure 7.4 shows how several Gaussian functions can be summed to produce a Gaussian kernel with a complex multipeaked pattern.

Figure 7.4: Gaussian Kernel

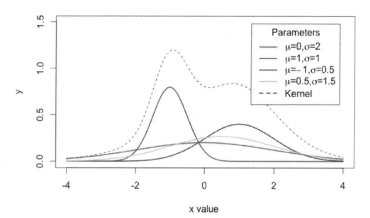

As you can see from the above graph, summing the individual Gaussian functions produces a Kernel that incorporates each of their peak values. The dotted line shows this kernel value.

7.2.1 Initial Candidate Solutions

The ACO initially places the ants at random locations. Each element of an ant's position (solution) vector is set to a random number between -1 and 1. The Gaussian kernels are not used to generate these random values, as the Gaussian kernels have not yet been established. The Gaussian kernels will be created based on the scores of this initial random population of ants.

The continuous ACO algorithm will employ a number of Gaussian kernels equal to the number of parameters that you are trying to optimize. If your RBF neural network had a parameter vector of length 10, you would use a separate Gaussian kernel to sample each element of the parameter vector. For each iteration, an ant moves to a new location based on the random numbers sampled from the Gaussian kernels. We must always store the position vector with the highest score. This highest scoring vector will become the ultimate solution of the continuous ACO.

7.2.2 Ant Movement

A typical Gaussian kernel will perform the summation of every component, as shown in Equation 7.5. A continuous ACO will only select one component Gaussian function at a time to calculate the elements of an ant's parameter vector. The continuous ACO chooses a mean and standard deviation for the elements of the solution vector. Using this mean and standard deviation, a new position is chosen for the elements of that ant's solution vector.

We will loop over every ant in the population and assign that ant a new location. Additionally, every ant in the population will have its own potentially unique model ant to help with the calculation. A roulette wheel selects the model ants based on desirability of that ant's score. Each ant will move towards its model ant's parameters.

We will use each of the model ant's solution vector elements as the mean values for the random Gaussian sample. We also need a standard deviation to generate a Gaussian random sample. Equation 7.6 calculates the standard deviation.

$$\sigma_l = \xi \sum_{i=1}^{N} \frac{x_i - x_l}{N-1} \qquad (7.6)$$

This equation bears some resemblance to the actual formula to calculate a sample's standard deviation; however, it was somewhat altered for the continuous ACO. Keep in mind that we are not calculating a standard deviation in the purest definition from statistics. We are calculating the value to use as the standard deviation parameter for random sampling from the Gaussian function.

Essentially, this equation calculates the mean difference between the model ant's parameter element (x sub l) and all of the other ants' parameter values (x sub i). We divide by N-1 because we do not want to include the model ant. The model ant's difference with itself is zero; so subtracting 1 from N effectively cancels it in both the numerator and denominator. You will also notice that Equation 7.6 includes the coefficient xi, which is analogous to the pheromone evaporation rate. This number should be between 0 and 1. The xi training parameter corresponds to the learning rate in many other training algorithms. High value for xi results in low convergence speed (Socha, 2007).

We will now examine the pseudocode necessary to implement ACO. Listing 7.6 shows the pseudocode for selecting a model ant.

Listing 7.6: Selecting a Model Ant

```
sub select_model_ant():
  l = 0

  # Calculate the total weighting (score) over all ants.
  sum_weighting = 0
  for each ant in ants:
    sum_weighting = sum_weighting + ant.weighting
  # Choose a random ant, with bias to better scoring ants.
  r = random_uniform()
  temp = 0
  # Loop over all ants using a roulette wheel selection.
  for each ant in ants:
    temp = temp + weighting[i] / sum_weighting
    if r < temp:
      return r
  # We should never reach this point.
  return -1
```

We will select a model ant for each of the ants that we must move. In addition to a model ant, we must also calculate the standard deviation in order to sample from the normal distribution. Listing 7.7 shows how to calculate the standard deviation.

Listing 7.7: Determine Standard Deviation

```
# Compute the standard deviation to use for random sampling.
sub compute_sd(ants, model_ant, x):
  # Sum the differences between the model ant and other ants.
  sum = 0.0
  for each ant in ants:
    sum = sum + abs(ant.params[x] - model_ant[x])
      / (length(ants)-1)
```

7.2 Continuous Ant Colony Optimization

```
# Force a minimum threshold.
if sum == 0:
  sum = MIN_SIGMA

# Apply evaporation rate and return.
return xi * sum
```

Apply the functions provided in Listings 7.6 and 7.7 to move all the ants. Listing 7.8 shows how the continuous ACO completes this process.

Listing 7.8: Continuous ACO Movement

```
def move_ants():
  # Loop over each ant in the population.
  for each ant in ants:

    # Choose the model ant.
    model_ant = select_model_ant()
    # Move the ant.
    for j from 0 to length(ant.params):
      # Determine the sigma and mu to sample a
      # random number from.
      sigma = compute_sd(ants, ants[model_ant], ants[j])
      mu = ant[pdf].params[j]
      # Sample the random number to become the ant's
      # new position.
      d = random_normal(mu, sigma)
      # Move this element of the ant's position.
      ants.params[j] = d
```

Continuous ACO can be applied to the RBF neural network iris model fitting process that we have seen with both particle swarm optimization (PSO) and genetic algorithms (GA). For fitting the iris data set, ACO tends to be the most efficient, followed by PSO and then GA. No general assumptions can be made across all data sets on algorithm efficiency. The fact that ACO performed best for the iris data set does not mean that ACO will perform the best for all data sets. The output from the ACO iris example is listed below.

```
Iteration #1, Score=0.20576496592647195,
Iteration #2, Score=0.20576496592647195,
Iteration #3, Score=0.20576496592647195,
...
Iteration #61, Score=0.05167890084491037,
```

```
Iteration #62, Score=0.05148646349444265,
Iteration #63, Score=0.047341109226974765,
Final score: 0.047341109226974765
[-0.55, 0.24, -0.86, -0.91] -> Iris-setosa, Ideal: Iris-setosa
[-0.66, -0.16, -0.86, -0.91] -> Iris-setosa, Ideal: Iris-setosa
...
[0.22, -0.16, 0.42, 0.58] -> Iris-virginica, Ideal: Iris-virginica
[0.05, 0.16, 0.49, 0.83] -> Iris-virginica, Ideal: Iris-virginica
[-0.11, -0.16, 0.38, 0.41] -> Iris-virginica, Ideal: Iris-
    virginica
```

As you can see, the ACO algorithm was able to fit the model in 63 iterations.

7.3 Chapter Summary

Ant colony optimization (ACO) is a cooperative population optimization algorithm. ACO works very similarly to a genetic algorithm because you can apply it to both discrete and continuous problems. ACO, particle swarm optimization (PSO), and genetic algorithms (GA) can be used interchangeably for continuous problems. However, PSO is not compatible with discrete problems, so only ACO and GA can be interchanged. Ultimately, selecting an algorithm is a programmer decision because no concrete rules exist for choosing one algorithm over another for a particular problem.

Discrete ACO was the first development of this algorithm. Determining optimal paths and orderings is the primary purpose of discrete ACO. The traveling salesman problem (TSP) and related path problems are a common use for discrete ACO, which works through simulated ants leaving pheromone trails. Successful ants reinforce good paths. Evaporation decreases pheromone strength and encourages ant exploration.

Continuous ACO allows the algorithm to optimize a vector of floating-point numbers by using a population of evolving probability distribution functions (PDF) that determine the next position for each ant. Calculating mean and standard deviation values from the population of ants shapes these PDFs.

Thus far, the focus of this book has been on cooperative and competitive populations that provide solutions to discrete and continuous problems.

7.3 Chapter Summary

Chapters 8 and 9 will focus on cellular automata and artificial life. Cellular automata apply simple rules to a grid of cells. Artificial life attempts to simulate simplified life forms.

Chapter 8

Cellular Automata

- Elementary Cellular Automation
- Conway's Game of Life
- Evolving Physics

Cellular automata (CA) are algorithms that manipulate values stored in grids or higher dimensional spaces. This chapter will focus on CAs in 2D spaces expressed as grids. As the cellular automation runs, it often produces complex animated patterns. However, the rules that govern the grid manipulations are usually very simple. Creating beautifully complex patterns with basic rules is the primary purpose of cellular automata.

Artificial life is a common application for cellular automata because individual grid cells can approximate actual cells. Consequently, video games frequently utilize them to enhance the entertainment experience. For example, cellular automata control water and lava flow in *Minecraft* (2009).

From a strictly business-oriented stand point, Chapters 8 and 9 are the least practical chapters in the book. Most of the algorithms presented in these chapters are for entertainment or artistic purposes. Nevertheless, cellular automata and artificial life are both very active areas of research. They were also very popular with the backers of this book's Kickstarter project. Chapters 8 and 9 do not contain any prerequisite knowledge for Chapter 10 or the remainder of this book series. If you are not interested in cellular automata or artificial life, you can skip to Chapter 10 without missing any prerequisite knowledge. Chapter 10 deals with data science, which is one of the most practical and popular applications of AI to business.

Although business applications rarely exploit cellular automata, other industries take advantage of this technology. Cryptography, simulation, random number generation, and music composition represent some of the applications for CA. To build your understanding of common cellular automata, this chapter will introduce elementary cellular automation and Conway's Game of Life. Finally, an example showing how to evolve your own cellular automata will conclude this chapter.

8.1 Elementary Cellular Automation

An elementary cellular automaton (ECA) is one-dimensional with two possible states (labeled 0 and 1). Often these states are shown graphically, with 0 as white and 1 as black. The rule to determine the state of a cell in the next generation depends only on the current state of the cell and its two immediate neighbors. As a result, ECA is one of the simplest possible cellular automata.

To create an ECA, start with a grid. The first row of the grid, called row 0, should be initialized either by all zeros, random values of 0 and 1, or a single 1 value in the center column. Row 1 will be initialized based on the values in row 0. Similarly, row 2 will be based on row 1. This process continues for as many rows as are present in the grid. To begin calculating row 1, we determine each pixel's value by looking at the three pixels immediately above the pixel we are considering. Figure 8.1 shows the three pixels that we consider from the previous row.

8.1 Elementary Cellular Automation

Figure 8.1: ECA Pixel Influencers

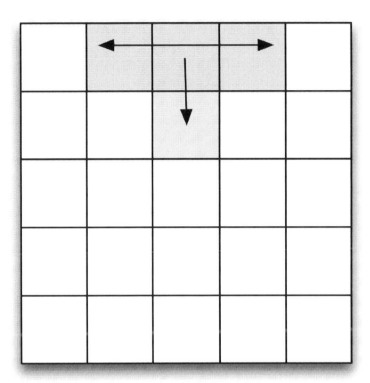

As you can see from the above figure, the pixel in row 1 (second row of the diagram) is influenced by the three shaded pixels above it in row 0 (first row of the diagram). A simple table defines how the previous three pixels influence the current pixel. If we have three bits, then we have eight possible combinations of values that we use to express the rules for the ECA. This process allows us to specify what the current pixel should be.

```
If previous row = 111 then current pixel = 0
If previous row = 110 then current pixel = 0
If previous row = 101 then current pixel = 0
If previous row = 100 then current pixel = 1
If previous row = 011 then current pixel = 1
If previous row = 010 then current pixel = 1
If previous row = 001 then current pixel = 1
If previous row = 000 then current pixel = 0
```

If we keep the order of the above if-statements constant, we can specify the behavior of an ECA with only the output bits. In this case, the above rules would simply be 00011110. Because eight values exist, there are two to the power of eight, or 256 combinations. In other words, we can specify a maximum of 256 different ECAs.

Steven Wolfram (2002) provided a standardized way of representing the rules of the ECA. The if-statements previously mentioned match the order of the if-statements that Wolfram established. Because of his view that binary numbers, such as 00011110, were too cumbersome to write, Wolfram opted for regular decimal numbers. The rules for the binary number 00011110 are called Rule 30 in Wolfram ECA notation. Rule 30 is shown graphically in Figure 8.2.

Figure 8.2: Wolfram's ECA Classification for Rule 30

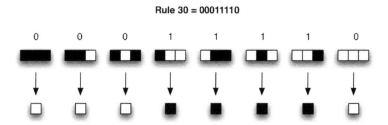

To run Rule 30, simply initialize the first row to a single 1 value in the middle column. Then loop over the next row and set each pixel to the requirements of Rule 30. When you calculate the first and last pixel of a row, you will be missing a left and right pixel from the previous row, respectively. Always assume missing pixels are zero. Figure 8.3 shows missing pixels at the edge of the grid.

8.1 Elementary Cellular Automation

Figure 8.3: Missing Pixels in a CA

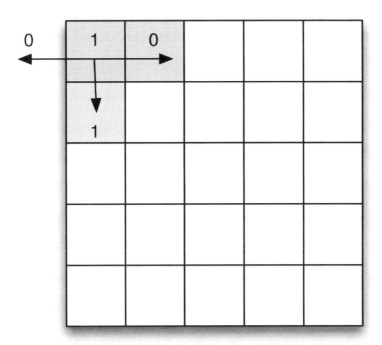

The above diagram shows the calculation of the first pixel of the second row. We have access to the pixel immediately north and northeast. However, the northwest pixel is missing and is treated as 0. Together with the north and northeast pixels, we have 010. According to Rule 30, this situation results in a value of 1. As expected, these rigid rules can produce highly repetitive patterns. The output from Rule 30 is shown in Figure 8.4.

Figure 8.4: Rule 30 ECA

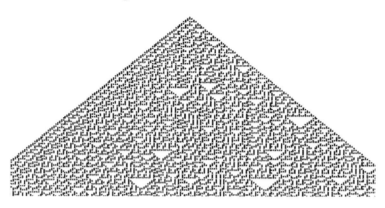

Because Rule 30 is a particularly interesting ECA, researchers have studied it extensively. It also occurs in nature. The triangles and line patterns that you see in Figure 8.4 appear on the shell, as seen in Figure 8.5.

Figure 8.5: Rule 30 in Nature

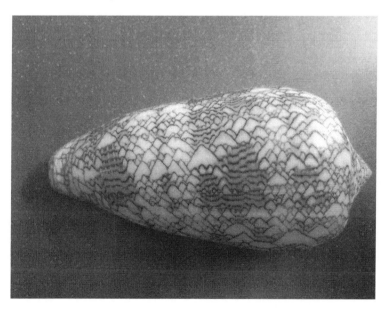

Not all ECA rules are as interesting as Rule 30. Figure 8.6 shows Rule 94, a highly repetitive ECA.

8.2 Conway's Game of Life

Figure 8.6: Rule 94 ECA

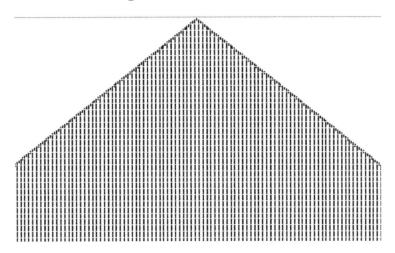

If you would like to see examples of other ECA rules, Steven Wolfram's website has images for all 256 rules.

http://mathworld.wolfram.com/ElementaryCellularAutomaton.html

8.2 Conway's Game of Life

Conway's Game of Life (1970) is one of the most well-known cellular automation programs. Unlike ECA, the Game of Life is a continuously running animation. The grid is updated after each iteration, and these iterations make the cells appear animated to the user. Figure 8.7 shows a single iteration of the Game of Life, using this book's JavaScript example.

Figure 8.7: Conway's Game of Life

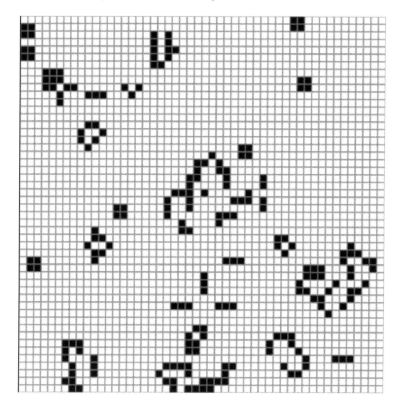

The above image really does not do justice to the Game of Life because it is not animated. You can see an animated version of the Game of Life at the following URL:

http://www.heatonresearch.com/fun/conway

The book's examples also contain animated versions of the Game of Life.

8.2 Conway's Game of Life

8.2.1 Rules of the Game of Life

Like most CAs, Conway's Game of Life follows a set of very simple, completely deterministic rules that lack randomness.

Listing 8.1: Rules of Conway's Game of Life

```
1. Any live cell with fewer than two live neighbors dies, as if
    caused by under-population.
2. Any live cell with two or three live neighbors lives on to the
    next generation. (The rule is not typically needed)
3. Any live cell with more than three live neighbors dies, as if
    by overcrowding.
4. Any dead cell with exactly three live neighbors becomes a live
    cell, as if by reproduction.
```

The above rules define a cell as a grid element containing the value 1. Rules 1 and 3 specify when a cell dies. Rule 2 regulates when a cell continues to live. Rule 4 determines when a new living cell is created. Setting the grid element to 1 creates a cell. Adjusting the grid element to 0 kills a cell.

Listing 8.1 displays the rules in the way that Conway originally stated. From a technical standpoint, rule 2 is not needed if you ignore the living cells that rules 1 and 3 do not cover. The examples provided for this book do not directly implement rule 3; living cells are left alive until another rule kills them.

Adherence to these rules will produce very complex animated patterns. Grids are usually initialized to random patterns. Running grids will often converge to a stable pattern. However, some grids can run for a very long time.

8.2.2 Interesting Life Patterns

Conway's Game of Life features many interesting patterns that researchers have already explored. You can study them and create worlds of your own through the free application Golly. Additionally, many published papers about the game's patterns cite Golly as a research tool. For this book, I captured Game of Life patterns with Golly. You can download the application from the following URL:

http://golly.sourceforge.net/

Some seemingly simple patterns can take a very long time to converge. Convergence refers to a grid that has reached a repeating state. The grid may still have movement, but it will cycle back to exactly the same state every 4 to 10 iterations. A pattern that takes a large number of iterations to converge is called a Methuselah. This name originates from a biblical character that reached the age of 969 years (Genesis 5:21-27). Figure 8.8 shows a relatively simple Methuselah.

Figure 8.8: The Blom Methuselah

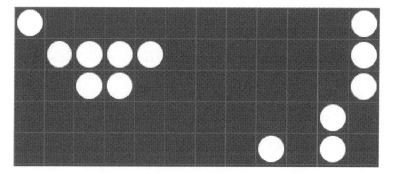

The above figure shows the Blom Methuselah that has a lifespan of 23,314 iterations before convergence (Hickerson, 2002). Once the cells reach this state, there are an average of 2,740 live cells. Most Methuselahs will shoot off spaceship-type particles as they age. These spaceships will travel indefinitely, and you should not count them as part of the convergence of the cellular automation.

8.2 Conway's Game of Life

A spaceship is a particle that retains its basic shape and moves in a fixed direction. Spaceships are a very interesting aspect of Game of Life research. One of the simplest spaceships is the glider in Figure 8.9.

Figure 8.9: Four Gliders

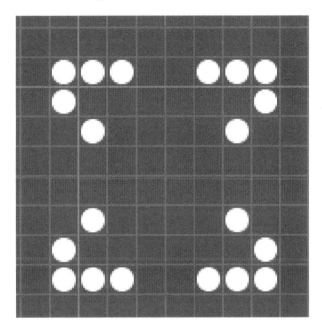

There are four gliders in the above figure. The top-left glider is moving northwest, the top-right glider is moving northeast, and the bottom two gliders are moving southwest and southeast, respectively. Gliders always fly diagonally, and the classic glider has only four different directions. All Game of Life spaceships travel by cycling through a series of phases. Figure 8.10 shows the four phases in a glider cycle.

Figure 8.10: The Four Glider Cycle Phases

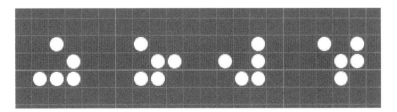

The glider flips through these four images much like the process of flipping pages to produce a cartoon. Additionally, spaceships can fly the four cardinal directions of north, south, east, and west. Another common pattern is the *glider gun* that can produce a stream of gliders in whatever direction the gun is pointed.

If you plot your Game of Life with Golly, a nearly infinite grid is put in effect. Because Golly stores the grid as a sparse 2D array, the memory only holds living cells. Figure 8.11 shows a Blom Methuselah after it has converged.

Figure 8.11: The Blom Methuselah from Afar

The above image displays a more distant view of the Methuselah. You should be able to see the converged Methuselah near the center of the image. Furthermore, dots radiate out to the northwest, northeast, southwest, and southeast. (The dots might be hard to see in some e-book forms of this book.) These dots are spaceships that were emitted while the Methuselah converged.

Scarcely any dots are in the northeast diagonal or near the core of Methuselah. One reason for this sparseness is the core becomes much less active as it ages. Only a few iterations had occurred after convergence when I took the screenshot. Eventually, the core would not have any nearby spaceships; they would all travel to deep space.

8.3 Evolve your Own Cellular Automata

Cellular automata like Conway's Game of Life are intriguing, and computer programmers have been experimenting with them since they were first introduced decades ago. I first saw Conway's Game of Life from the Loadstar monthly disc subscription for Commodore 64. Although the program was painfully slow and could support only a grid the size of the C64's 40x25 screen, it fascinated me. I translated the slow BASIC code to much faster 6510 assembly language.

Conway's four simple rules inspired me, and I wanted to create my own cellular automation. We've already seen that we can evolve programs using evolutionary algorithms. I will now show you how to evolve your own unique cellular automata.

In this section, I will introduce you to a cellular automation that I created called merge physics. This original research cellular automation is published to Code Project (http://www.codeproject.com). Merge physics, my highest-rated Code Project article, can be found at the following URL:

http://goo.gl/RwNKqw

The goal of merge physics is to produce new and interesting cellular automata using a very simple cellular automation. Therefore, I define a cellular automation similar to ECA. Instead of a single 8-bit number to tweak, I utilize a vector of 16 floating-point numbers. Different combinations of these numeric constants can produce some very impressive patterns.

Obviously, optimizing floating-point vectors is a primary focus of this book. However, the scoring function is not so simple. To evolve these CAs, human-based genetic algorithms (HBGA) are necessary. As the name implies, an

HBGA requires a human to fulfill parts of the genetic algorithm (GA). The user's job is to determine which cellular automata look interesting. The user ultimately fulfills the role of the score function.

Here is a very simple pattern vector that produces slowly growing purple blobs that are enclosed by a membrane and lack an internal structure. This universe ultimately converges to a stable pattern. Figure 8.12 shows this pattern.

Figure 8.12: Simple Stable Merge Physics Universe

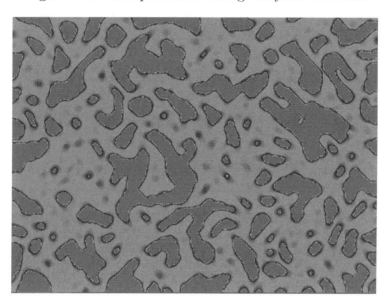

The vector that produces this purple blob universe is shown here. (Note: if you save this vector to a file to open in the multiverse viewer, make sure there are no line breaks.)

```
[0.8500022604957287, −0.018862014555296902,
−0.5920368462156294, 0.6025118473507605,
−0.25332713280631114, −0.9442865152657809,
0.8385370421691785, 0.11515083295327955,
0.07865610718434457, −0.4461260674309575,
0.6233523022386354, −0.10991833670148407,
0.9372981778896297, 0.7423301656036665,
0.1214234643293226, 0.02417402657410897]
```

8.3 Evolve your Own Cellular Automata

The red universe that follows is one of my favorites so far. A lot of activity takes place in this universe that resembles a colorful version of Conway's Game of Life. Spaceships, guns and rakes abound! A rake is a type of spaceship that leaves behind a trail of debris. The universe is very busy and rarely converges to a static state. Cellular structures also appear to move randomly. However, only the initial state is random. Everything else in merge physics is deterministic. You can observe the red universe in Figure 8.13.

Figure 8.13: The Red Universe

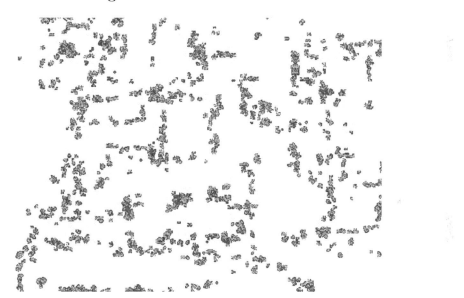

You might be wondering why I call Figure 8.13 the "red universe" when it contains very little red. Because some versions of this book are printed in black and white, I replaced the red background in Figure 8.13 with white for aesthetic reasons.

The vector that produces the "red universe" is shown here.

[0.7975713097932856, 0.04290606443410394,
−0.24797271002387022, 0.9078879446367496,
0.15307785453690795, 0.023971186791761356,
0.9064792766828782, −0.5248003131303094,
−0.1456779635182246, 0.6998501852403781,
−0.0026800425987849597, −0.8630977046192441,
0.06143751170130951, 0.8228374543146946,
−0.11483923870647716, 0.6399758923339068]

Figure 8.14 shows a yellow universe that is very cell-like.

Figure 8.14: Yellow Cellular Universe

I removed the yellow background from the previous universe to support black and white versions of this book. The cells have defined membranes and are in motion. Unlike the red universe (Figure 8.13), the cells do not move in strict horizontal or vertical directions. On the contrary, their movement is much more erratic in all directions.

8.3 Evolve your Own Cellular Automata

Figures 8.12 through 8.14 do not do justice to their universes since they lack animation. The following YouTube video features the animated universes:

http://www.youtube.com/watch?v=Vphx4sYcI-o

The above video also provides an introduction to the multiverse viewer example program in this section. This viewer displays several universes close together so you can choose the most compelling ones for the genetic algorithm.

8.3.1 Understanding Merge Physics

Different terms often describe cellular automata and genetic algorithms. The following definitions of these terms will help you understand this article:

- **Cell:** One "grid square" in a universe. Each cell has a 3-sized vector that represents an RGB color. Each element of this vector ranges between -1 and 1. The value -1 means the color component is fully off, whereas the value of 1 means the color component is fully on.

- **Crossover**: When two parents produce children that contain some elements from both parents.

- **Genome**: One life form in a genetic algorithm's population. Genomes are usually vectors of a fixed length. For this article, genomes have physics vectors of size 16.

- **Mutation**: When a single parent produces a child. The offspring genome vector will contain a vector that represents a slight distortion of the single parent.

- **Physics**: The rules that govern how the universe changes each time frame. The physics of a universe is defined by 16 physical constants that are stored in a vector.

- **Time Frame**: A universe's physics is run once per time frame. The screen is updated at the end of each time frame.

- **Universe**: A grid of cells that are usually initialized to random pixels. Each universe must have physics that define how it changes each time frame.

The merge physics universe is essentially a grid of pixels or cells. Unlike Conway's Game of Life, individual cells are not simply on or off. They contain red, green, and blue vectors. Each cell has one numeric vector where each component is in the range -1 to 1. A value of -1 means that the color component is fully off, whereas a value of 1 means the color component is fully on. For example, white would be **[1,1,1]** and black would be **[-1,-1,-1]**. Blue would be **[-1,-1,1]**. Figure 8.15 shows this universe.

Figure 8.15: The Merge Physics Universe

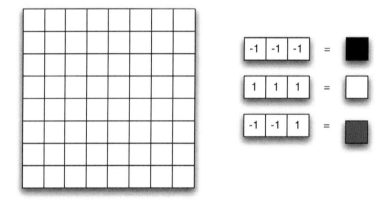

This configuration allows the universe to represent any of the RBG colors. Typically, the programmer initializes the universe to random color values by setting each cell to a vector of three random numbers between -1 and 1.

The physics works by adjusting each pixel value during a time frame. Each pixel is merged with a particular key color. A vector of 16 values defines the exact means by which this merging happens. These 16 values are the universal constants that define a universe's physics. Changing these 16 values can create many different universes. Some are very simple and quickly stabilize to a single color. Others are more enthralling and produce complex patterns.

8.3 Evolve your Own Cellular Automata

All physical constants must be between -1 and 1. You can think of these 16 vector constants in the following manner:

[v0 , v1 , v2 , v3 , v4 , v5 , v6 , v7 , v8 , v9 , v10 , v11 , v12 , v13 , v14 , v15]

Figure 8.16 shows how these constants map to their key colors.

Figure 8.16: Merge Physics Vector Layout

Index	Red	Green	Blue	Resulting Color	Limit	Percent
0	-1	-1	-1	Black	v0	v1
1	1	-1	-1	Red	v2	v3
2	-1	1	-1	Green	v4	v5
3	1	1	-1	Yellow	v6	v7
4	-1	-1	1	Blue	v8	v9
5	1	-1	1	Purple	v10	v11
6	-1	1	1	Cyan	v12	v13
7	1	1	1	White	v14	v15

The 16 physical constants are actually 8 pairs for each of the 8 key colors. The key colors are black, red, green, yellow, blue, purple, cyan, and white. The above chart shows the key colors in order by their index. The red, green, and blue columns show the values for the RGB components. Just like the universe pixels, -1 is full off and 1 is full on. The resulting color is shown in the fifth column. The last two columns show the vector indexes for each of the key color's limit and percent. These values come from the physical constants vector.

Each color pixel is considered 1 by 1. The algorithm also determines the average value of all eight of the pixel's neighbors, which are grid elements immediately N, S, E, W, NE, NW, SW or SE of the current pixel. If the pixels are on an edge, then a vector of three zeros is used for that pixel. This setting works well because zero is the mean of -1 and 1, and the program calculates it across the color components of all neighbor pixels. The following equation determines the mean of the color vectors of the neighbors:

$$\mu = \frac{\sum_{i=1}^{N} r_i + g_i + b_i}{3N} \tag{8.1}$$

N is the number of neighbors. N is typically 8; however, you can decrease it for edge pixels. You can also consider the off-grid pixels as zeros. Both approaches for handling the pixels on the edge are mathematically equivalent.

The calculated value for the mean (mu) determines the direction that the key color moves. We consider each of the key colors in the order of their limit values. Once we find a key color with a higher limit value than the mean, we know the target key color. Next, the percent value (from the physical constant vector) sets the distance of the key color we should move. If the percent value is -1, then the current pixel will not change. If the percent value is 1, then the current pixel will immediately obtain the value of the key color. The percentages are stored in the range -1 to 1, so you should denormalize them to actual percent values. You can accomplish this simple process with the following formula:

$$p = \frac{x+1}{2} \tag{8.2}$$

The same value p is used for red, green, and blue. Equation 8.3 shows how we finally determine the value for the new cell (c), or pixel, based on the percent (p) for the red (r), green (g) and blue (b) values. We are basically moving the pixel vector towards the key color (k).

$$c_{n+1} = [r_n + p(r_k - r_n), g_n + p(g_k - g_n), b_n + p(b_k - b_n)] \tag{8.3}$$

This section has an example of the multiverse viewer. Some of the programming languages in the examples execute many adjacent universes through multithreading. Whether an example uses multithreading depends on the programming language in the example. Refer to the README file to see whether the examples for each language support multithreading.

Genetic algorithm constructs can create new universes. Start with a set of random universes, and the user can kill off more common universes. As a result, multiple, dynamic universes can mate and create a descendant universe. A single dynamic universe can create offspring that are mutated versions of the parent. The multithreaded code allows several universes to run fairly quickly on a multicore machine.

8.4 Chapter Summary

This chapter introduced cellular automata (CA) that modify grids based on a simple set of rules. Most CAs are created primarily for entertainment to produce animated effects. However, CAs can also have more practical applications, such as simulation, optimization, and cryptography. CAs can exist in higher dimensions spaces; however, this book focuses on CAs in 2D grids.

Elementary cellular automata (ECA) are a set of 256 simple CAs based on a rule number. Many of these CAs are highly repetitive; however, some rules produce very unique patterns. ECAs create a single static image without any animation. Some ECAs also generate random numbers in the computer program *Mathematica*.

Conway's Game of Life is an animated CA that has garnered a lot of attention since its introduction in 1970 because it can produce very complex patterns with a simple set of four rules. A variety of patterns have been discovered for the Game of Life that includes gliders, space ships, guns, and other objects.

Merge physics is a simple cellular automaton that I created in 2014. It allows you to evolve your own CA through a human-based genetic algorithm (HBGA). The user receives a variety of CAs and can choose his favorites for crossover and mutation.

In the next chapter, we will build upon cellular automata and introduce artificial life (ALIFE). I will demonstrate an ALIFE application that allows plants to evolve to take better advantage of limited resources, such as sunlight and water.

Chapter 9

Artificial Life

- Capstone Projects
- Drawing a Plant
- Animating Plant Growth
- Evolving the Ultimate Seed

I launched this book as a Kickstarter project, and backers could choose a capstone project as one of the rewards. A capstone project is a lengthy example that utilizes many of the techniques in this book. Backers suggested several projects and ultimately chose an artificial life project. Because my Kickstarter supporters also expressed considerable interest in a data science capstone project, Chapter 10 features a modeling capstone. Furthermore, I will present this project in three parts to reflect the program's stages as I developed them.

The Chapter 9 project is the design of an artificial plant box that allows a seed to grow to a fully mature plant. In addition to the example source code, I include my solution to this project. The program generates seeds that become superior plants because of an evolutionary algorithm. The seed begins with three living cells and follows an evolvable set of rules that govern the type of plant produced. Figure 9.1 shows a plant grown from this program.

Figure 9.1: Finished Version of the Plant Box

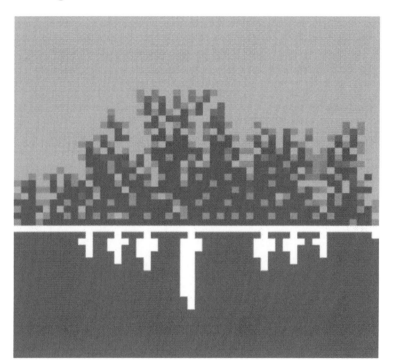

As you can see from the above figure, a full-grown plant includes leaves, stems, and a root system. The above plant evolved over several hundred generations.

To create this project, I completed three milestones that I discuss in later sections of this chapter. Specifically, I will provide an overview of these milestones as well as describe the challenges that I encountered. If you want to see the exact implementation of any part of this project, refer to the source code examples for this book.

I intend for this section to be a possible starting point for your own artificial life project. I hope that my program will give you some ideas for your own projects. To begin, I typically have a general plan of what I want to evolve. However, if I am going to evolve a plant, my approach is somewhat different from the moving cells in Chapter 8. I like to nudge the universe in the desired direction, but I also want to give it latitude to grow into something that might surprise me. This process is often trial and error until the universe evolves something worthwhile.

9.1 Milestone 1: Drawing a Plant

For the first part of this project, we simply display the seed that will grow into a plant. No matter how they evolve, all plants in the project will start from the same seed. As we see in Figure 9.2, this seed will occupy three vertical grid cells of the universe grid.

Figure 9.2: Seed

To render the previous image, the universe must contain a rectangular grid that is 50-wide by 100-high. Each grid cell in this universe has the following attributes that determine its appearance:

- **Leafiness**: This affects how green (leaf) or brown (trunk) is the cell. 1.0 is fully leaf, 0.0 is fully trunk.

- **Energy**: This defines the amount of energy between [0 and 1]. A dead cell is 0.

- **Nourishment**: This shows the amount of nourishment between [0 and 1].

- **Calculated Sunlight**: This indicates the calculated sunlight exposure.

- **Calculated Water**: This measures the calculated water exposure.

9.1 Milestone 1: Drawing a Plant

A cell is dead if the **energy** value is 0. As a result, the cell appears transparent. In other words, blue will show if the cell is above the horizon. If it is below the horizon, the cell will have the color of soil. The default settings for the horizon, or ground line, are two-thirds down from the top, or 66 pixels. If energy is present, then the cell will display a value between brown and green depending on the **leafiness** attribute. Grid cells below the ground line are roots, and the program must always draw them as pure white.

As you can see from Figure 9.2, the seed consists of the following three parts: root, stem, and leaf. The root is one unit below the ground level; the stem is right at ground level, and the leaf is one unit above ground level. The leaf has a maximum leafiness value, and the stem is halfway between leafy and trunk.

- Leafiness (for root): 0
- Nourishment (for root): 1
- Energy (for root): 1
- Leafiness (for stem): 0.5
- Nourishment (for stem): 1
- Energy (for stem): 1
- Leafiness (for leaf): 0
- Nourishment (for leaf): 1
- Energy (for leaf): 1

All other cells in the grid should have all attributes set to 0. This information should help you create a program that displays Figure 9.2. If you need more guidance, refer to the capstone examples that have many relevant comments.

To draw the plant, you must determine the color for every living cell. As a result, you need a palette of several combinations of red, green, and blue (RGB).

- Fully leafy color (greenish) = [0, 255, 0]
- Fully stem color (brownish) = [165, 42, 42]
- Sky color (bluish) = [135, 206, 250]
- Dirt color (grayish) = [96, 96, 96]
- Root color (white) = [255,255,255]

The above colors specify the values of the RGB vector [red, blue, green]. The RGB components range from 0-255. Any part of the plant below ground simply has the root color. The gradient between the fully leafy and stem colors affects the parts of the plant above ground. The leafiness attribute, which determines the pixel's distance between the stem and leafy color, is necessary to calculate the gradient. Furthermore, these values are ideal to prepopulate a table. The pseudocode in Listing 9.1 shows these values in action.

Listing 9.1: Generate Leafiness Gradient

```
# Calculate the ranges we must cover.
gradentRangeRed = LEAF_GREEN.red - STEM_BROWN.red
gradentRangeGreen = LEAF_GREEN.green - STEM_BROWN.green
gradentRangeBlue = LEAF_GREEN.blue - STEM_BROWN.blue
# Determine the maximum range between red, green & blue.
maxRange = max(max(
  abs(gradentRangeRed),
  abs(gradentRangeGreen)),
  abs(gradentRangeBlue));
# Scale each of the color ranges to this maximum range.
# Because each color component has a different range, it is
# necessary to move by a different amount in each RGB component.
scaleRed = (double) gradentRangeRed / (double) maxRange;
scaleGreen = (double) gradentRangeGreen / (double) maxRange;
scaleBlue = (double) gradentRangeBlue / (double) maxRange;
# Create an array to hold the gradient colors
gradient = new [maxRange];
```

```
# Calculate the gradients
for i from 0 to maxRange-1:
  gradient[i] = new Color(
    int (STEM_BROWN.getRed() + (i * scaleRed)),
    int (STEM_BROWN.getGreen() + (i * scaleGreen)),
    int (STEM_BROWN.getBlue() + (i * scaleBlue)))
```

Once the above code completes, you now have a gradient color table stored in the gradient variable. Because the leafiness attribute is a percent, you can determine the appropriate color by multiplying leafiness by the length of the table.

9.2 Milestone 2: Animating Plant Growth

The first milestone created a program capable of drawing a plant universe grid. Animation is rapidly drawing a series of frames. For the second milestone, you will create an animated plant that allows you to observe its growth from a seed to a full-grown plant as seen in Figure 9.3.

Figure 9.3: Growing Plant

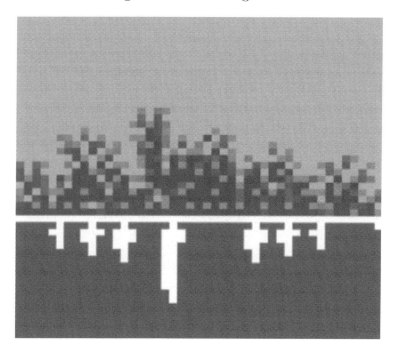

The above figure shows only a single frame of the entire growth sequence. The following URL has a video of a plant growing and one of seeds evolving in the third milestone.

https://www.youtube.com/watch?v=-eC-PyCMwn0

To accomplish this animation, you will need two different systems working together. First, a physics system controls the plant structural integrity, light, water absorption, and nutrient circulation inside of the plant. Second, the plant growth system manages its development based on the plant's DNA vector.

9.2.1 Plant Physics

The physics class defines limits on the growth that the plant's DNA wants to implement. It is important to keep the physics as simple as possible. Because

9.2 Milestone 2: Animating Plant Growth

the plants have evolutionary capabilities, they should be able to evolve into a reasonable universe. However, some tweaking might be necessary to define the universe's physical characteristics. Without these adjustments, your universe will not produce life.

Overall, I was able to keep the physics relatively simple for this universe. However, controlling the circulation while forcing the plant to grow roots was difficult for my design. I also had to make some adjustments in order to attain a good ratio of shade that would produce nice, leafy plants that were not too green in areas away from the sun.

Physics determines how the plant absorbs sunlight and distributes nourishment. The growth process of the cell mimics nature. Cells acquire sunlight from above, and the light stops at the ground level. More leafy material absorbs sunlight and reduces it because of shade. Less leafy material provides less shade and can circulate energy and nourishment better. Additionally, the cells obtain water from an underground stream. For the sake of simplicity, the stream is the only source of water. The deeper the roots grow, the more water they receive. Thus, the values for these growth phases of the cells are **calculated energy** and **nourishment** values, and they represent the actual energy produced from sunlight as well as the nourishment provided by water. Each cell stores these values for its growth phases.

The physics engine allows you to determine water and light distribution. You calculate light in a top-down manner with the strongest light at the top of the universe rectangle. The program creates a vector with a width equal to the width of the universe and initializes all values to 1. This vector represents the strength of light, and each value in the vector will decrease as the plant absorbs the light. You calculate water with a bottom-up method, just like light. Figure 9.4 shows the sun and water vectors.

Figure 9.4: Sun and Water

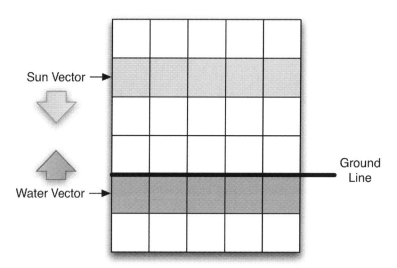

The program performs the sun and water calculations in two separate passes. The sunlight pass occurs first, followed by the water passes. Both passes run the entire height of the grid. However, once the sunlight vector crosses the ground level, it becomes all zeros. Likewise, once the water vector crosses the ground line, it reduces completely to zero.

Shade decreases the value of each element of the light vector that crosses a living grid cell. The amount of decay is equal to the leafiness times 0.1. For example, if a light vector element of 0.5 crossed a living cell with a leafiness of 0.9, we would multiply 0.9 by 0.1 and obtain a decay of 0.09. Then we would multiply the light vector value of 0.5 by 0.09. The subsequent decay value of 0.09 would reduce the 0.5 light vector value to only 0.045. This same process occurs for water.

The decay discussed in the previous section accounts for shade and water absorption; however, it does not deal with circulation in the plant. Even though the sun and water vectors translate into energy and nourishment for the plant, individual cells can also receive energy and nourishment through circulation. This process allows energy from the sun to reach the roots and nourishment from the ground to reach the leaves. Figure 9.5 shows circulation.

9.2 Milestone 2: Animating Plant Growth

Figure 9.5: Plant Circulation

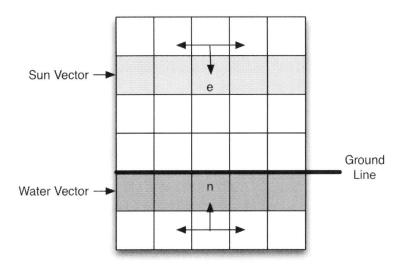

The above figure demonstrates how we calculate the energy, labeled **e**, and the nourishment, labeled **n**. Each living grid cell calculates the energy and nourishment from circulation. The energy from circulation (**e**) is the maximum-calculated energy from the three cells immediately above it. In the same way, the nourishment (**n**) from circulation is the maximum-calculated nourishment from the three grid cells below. The program counts only living grid cells in these maximums. The current cell's calculated nourishment will be set to the maximum of the circulation nourishment and the water vector. Additionally, you need to set the calculated energy for a cell to the maximum of the sunlight vector and the calculated energy. Cells will die if their nourishment drops below a threshold value.

For the sake of simplicity, circulation moves in a single direction. Nourishment goes up while energy goes down, as seen in Figure 9.5. Circulation presented a challenge for this project. On one hand, I did not want overly complex circulation physics. On the other hand, eliminating circulation would remove the reason to create stems and trunks. Consequently, I experimented with several methods of circulation. The best tradeoff between complexity and the forced evolution of stems and trunks was the final method that I tried. The above figure illustrates this method.

Another challenge was creating enough roots to support the plant. If we did not introduce a root limitation, a single root would be sufficient to nourish the entire plant. The sun pass counts the number of plant cells above ground, and the water pass counts the number of living plant cells below ground. Growth will only occur if the root ratio supports it. The next section contains the exact process to calculate the root ratio.

9.2.2 Plant Growth

For the second milestone, you will need to provide a plant DNA vector. Listing 9.2 shows an effective DNA vector.

Listing 9.2: Sample Plant Vector

```
[ 0.08414097456375995, 0.11845586131703176,
0.1868971940834313, 0.4346911204161327,
0.024190631402031804, 0.5773526701833149,
0.8997253827355136, 0.9267311086327318,
0.04639229538493471, 0.8190692654645835,
0.06531672676605614, 0.026431639742068264,
0.31497914852215286, 1.0276526539348398,
0.03303133293309127, 0.35946010922382937]
```

Figure 9.1, previously mentioned, shows the final growth of the plant. The plant DNA vector is essentially the program that the plant runs to determine how it should grow. Ultimately, the physics that we saw in the previous section limits the plant's development because it must support growth in a way that provides proper energy and nourishment.

A plant genome is an array of four vectors that has a length of 4. Therefore, the entire genome is 4*4 = 16 values. Each of the four vectors corresponds to a cell's DNA vector. A cell info vector provides information about the state of a grid cell. The grid cell can be either living (filled) or dead (empty).

9.2 Milestone 2: Animating Plant Growth

The four numeric elements of each of the vectors contained in the plant's DNA vector are the following:

- Element 0: The height of the cell. 1.0 for the last row and 0.0 for the first row.
- Element 1: The amount of sunlight (for surface cells) or water (for underground cells) exposure for this cell.
- Element 2: Crowding by neighbors.
- Element 3: Nourishment for this cell.

The four vectors, composed of the elements described in the previous section, are shown here.

- Vector 0: Stem desired
- Vector 1: Leaf desired
- Vector 2: Growth option #1
- Vector 3: Growth option #2

Vectors 0 and 1 go together. For each living cell, we determine if its info vector is closer to vector 0 or vector 1. If it is closer to stem (0), then we decrease the leafiness attribute of the cell. Leaves can only move towards the stem. However, a stem cannot change back into a leaf. Vectors 2 and 3 also go together. When a plant cell is eligible for growth, it evaluates all neighbor cells to select where it wants to grow. Thus, it chooses the neighbor cell that is closest to either vector 2 or 3. No growth occurs if the candidate cell is not lower than a specific threshold of vector 2 or 3.

For growth to occur, the program must maintain a ratio between the leafy surface portion and the roots. This ratio is calculated as follows:

```
root ratio = sum(root nourishment) / sum(leafiness)
```

If this ratio is less than 0.5, then roots can grow. If this ratio is above 0.5, then surface growth is allowed. This ratio ensures that the roots can sufficiently support the surface plant.

To perform the growth, we loop over every grid cell in the universe.

9.3 Milestone 3: Evolving a Plant

Evolutionary algorithms, such as genetic algorithms, particle swarm optimization, and ant colony optimization, can evolve the DNA vector that grows plants. To learn how to produce better plant DNA vectors, the previous volume of this series contains examples of optimization algorithms like simulated annealing and Nelder-Mead.

This project uses a genetic algorithm, as introduced in Chapter 3. The GA population model matches our goal of simulating a population of plants that evolves to produce the best plant. When you run the example for this milestone, you will see an ever evolving plant that represents the best plant found so far, as seen in Figure 9.6.

9.3 Milestone 3: Evolving a Plant

Figure 9.6: Evolving a Plant

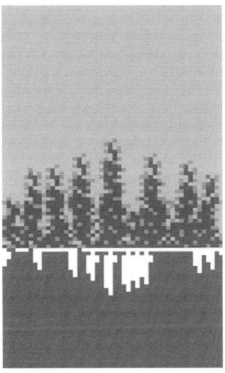

The above plant is midway through its evolutionary process and will further improve. This example will run indefinitely and print out the DNA vector of the top plant for each generation. Of course, the above plant is only on generation 11 and will improve considerably with subsequent generations.

9.3.1 Scoring a Plant

A scoring function is the process that determines the quality of a particular plant. This algorithm is very simple; the greener the plant is, the higher the score. Plants have 100 cycles to grow before the program evaluates their greenness. Listing 9.3 shows the pseudocode that scores a plant.

Listing 9.3: Plant Scoring

```
score = 0
count = 0
# Assume that universe contains cells after 100
# cycles of a particular plant growing.
for each cell in universe:
  if cell is alive:
    count = count + 1
    if cell is root:
# Give partial credit for a root
      score = score + 0.5;
    else:
      score = score + cell.leafiness
# Calculate average leafiness and roots
score = score / count
```

The score is the average leafiness by living cell, with roots counting as 0.5. Even though branches with low leafiness do not help the score, they are necessary because they move energy and nourishment around the plant. This is just one approach to scoring the plant, and the score function should be designed to create whatever type of organism you desire.

9.4 Chapter Summary

Artificial life is the simulation of living organisms with a computer. Research and entertainment applications frequently utilize artificial life. The cellular automata in the last chapter are a somewhat restricted form of artificial life. The capstone project for this chapter takes many concepts from cellular automata and combines them with the evolutionary algorithms from earlier chapters.

This capstone project featured a plant simulation. A fixed-length vector served the role of plant's DNA. A physics component detailing the collec-

9.4 Chapter Summary

tion and circulation parameters for energy and nourishment constrained the growth. Ultimately, the physics limits the plant's growth potential. The successful plants evolve because they can maximize growth within the restrictions established by physics.

This chapter introduced a capstone project and demonstrated the synthesis of material from the entire book. Although artificial life is a fascinating area of research, day-to-day business operations rarely take advantage of its possibilities. Data science, on the other hand, is an area in which many AI techniques can be applied for practical business scenarios. Thus, Chapter 10 will introduce a data science capstone project that highlights one of these applications.

Chapter 10

Modeling

- Kaggle Competitions
- Data Science
- Titanic Data
- Cross-validation

The capstone project from Chapter 9 demonstrated an application of nature-inspired algorithms for entertainment or simulation. This chapter will present a capstone project on modeling, a business-oriented use for artificial intelligence and part of a much broader field called data science.

Because data science is a relatively new field, it can be difficult to define. Drew Conway (2013), a leading data scientist, defines it as the intersection of the three fields: hacking skills, math and statistics knowledge, and substantive expertise. Figure 10.1 depicts this definition.

Figure 10.1: Conway's Data Science Venn Diagram

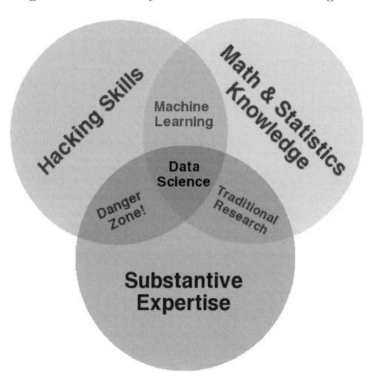

Hacking skills are essentially a subset of computer programming. Although data scientist does not necessarily need the infrastructure knowledge of an information technology (IT) professional, these technical skills will permit him or her to create short, effective programs for processing data. In the field of data science, information processing is called data wrangling.

Math and statistics knowledge covers statistics, probability, and other inferential methods. Substantive knowledge describes the business knowledge as well as the comprehension of actual data. If you combine only two of these topics, you don't have all the components for data science, as Figure 10.1 illustrates. In other words, the combination of statistics and substantive expertise is simply traditional research. Those two skills alone don't encompass the capabilities (i.e., machine learning) required for data science.

My book series deals with hacking skills and math and statistical knowledge, two of the circles in Figure 10.1. Additionally, it teaches you to create your own models, which is more pertinent to the field of computer science than data science. Substantive expertise is more difficult to obtain because it is dependent on the industry that utilizes the data science applications. For example, if you want to apply data science in the insurance industry, substantive knowledge refers to the actual business operations of these companies.

10.1 Competitive Data Science

To demonstrate this field of technology, I need data. Kaggle, a website that hosts data science competitions, is a good source of data.

http://www.kaggle.com

Kaggle runs competitions in which data scientists compete in order to provide the best model to fit the data. The capstone project of this chapter features Kaggle's Titanic data set. The following URL has the Titanic completion:

https://www.kaggle.com/c/titanic-gettingStarted

Before we get started with the Titanic example, it's important to be aware of some Kaggle guidelines. First, most competitions end on a specific date. Website organizers have currently scheduled the Titanic competition to end on December 31, 2014. However, they have already extended the deadline several times, and an extension beyond 2014 is also possible. Second, the Titanic data set is considered a tutorial data set. In other words, there is no prize, and your score in the competition does not count towards becoming a Kaggle Master. To achieve the highest rank, you must compete in three Kaggle competitions, place in the top 10 of a competition once, and score in the top 10% twice. Each Kaggle completion has a leaderboard that shows the top contenders. Figure 10.2 depicts the Titanic leaderboard from July 15, 2014.

Figure 10.2: Kaggle Leaderboard

#	Δ1w	Team Name *in the money	Score	Entries	Last Submission UTC (Best - Last Submission)
1	—	Koby Karp *	1.00000	1	Wed, 21 May 2014 18:14:09
2	—	Min-Sik Park	1.00000	15	Sun, 25 May 2014 08:19:21 (-6.2h)
3	—	Hanemori	1.00000	62	Mon, 02 Jun 2014 07:52:26 (-25.2h)
4	—	timothy235	1.00000	6	Fri, 06 Jun 2014 17:00:23
5	—	DG_IST565	1.00000	37	Fri, 11 Jul 2014 23:15:03 (-26.2d)
6	—	John Uckele	1.00000	18	Fri, 27 Jun 2014 18:31:21 (-7.3d)
7	—	Henry Bowers	0.99522	1	Mon, 26 May 2014 16:49:04
8	—	Moti Mizrahi	0.99043	78	Thu, 19 Jun 2014 14:44:07 (-18.7d)
9	—	DataMatrix	0.98086	1	Wed, 02 Jul 2014 11:25:27
10	—	LazyBoy145	0.97608	12	Fri, 23 May 2014 02:51:41

Kaggle scores competitions in a variety of ways. The Titanic competition gives you a set of passengers, and you must predict whether they lived or died. The previous scores represent the percentage of passengers that you succeed in predicting. A score of 1.0 is perfect accuracy, and a score of 0.5 means that half of your predictions were incorrect.

Furthermore, Kaggle gives you two CSV files named *test* and *train*. Both files give you attributes, often called features, about the passengers. The *train* file provides the outcome that you are trying to forecast. As you work with the Titanic problem, you can build your model with the *train* data set. However, the *test* data set is essentially a quiz; you fill in the answers to be graded. Once you complete your predictions for the *test* data set and submit it, Kaggle scores your work.

As you can observe from Figure 10.2, Kaggle allows multiple submissions. Although you work with the same *test* data, you receive a different score every time that you submit. Kaggle also places a limit on the number of submissions per day. Because the *test* data usually contain a lot of rows, brute-force guessing will not be productive. Additionally, Kaggle administrators view the registration of multiple accounts for the purpose of gaining more daily submissions as cheating, and they strictly enforce the rule, occasionally disqualifying individuals for this behavior.

10.1 Competitive Data Science

The leaderboard also displays some competitors who received a perfect 1.0 score in the Titanic competition. Nevertheless, their achievement is questionable because Wikipedia contains a complete list of Titanic passengers and their fates that anyone can easily search.

http://en.wikipedia.org/wiki/Passengers_of_the_RMS_Titanic

Consequently, even without programming skills, you could receive a perfect score by simply marking the correct outcome in the test data after you researched the passengers' fates in Wikipedia. It's important to remember, though, that the Titanic data set is a tutorial, not an actual competition. The general consensus in Kaggle's Titanic forums is that any score above 85% has been manipulated with previously published information.

In other words, predicting with great accuracy every passenger's fate is not possible because the final hours of Titanic were extremely chaotic. Although women with higher-classed tickets had the best chances of survival, accidents may have occurred or panicked passengers may not have reached a lifeboat. Thus, individuals with a completely unpredictable outcome are called outliers.

Lifeboat #1 added a number of outliers. Although this lifeboat had 40 seats, it launched with just 12 people. Two passengers aboard were women, and there were no children. Once news spread about this disparity, Lifeboat #1 caused a lot of controversy, and allegations of bribery surfaced. Therefore, no reasonable model could predict the outcome of the occupants of Lifeboat #1. For example, John Jacob Astor, one of the richest men in 1912, was a prominent Titanic victim. Given the alleged bribery of the crew, Astor should have been a survivor in Lifeboat #1. However, he was denied a seat on another lifeboat despite his request to evacuate with his pregnant wife. To solve the dilemma of Lifeboat #1, an overfit model might learn to predict the outcomes of the passengers. However, you should avoid overfitting because the model has only memorized parts of the data. We want to create a model that learns from the data; one that memorizes data is useless.

10.2 Milestone 1: Wrangling the Data

Data are very rarely in a form that a model can use. Listing 10.1 exemplifies this fact as it shows the beginning of the Titanic training data.

Listing 10.1: Titanic Training Data

```
PassengerId,Survived,Pclass,Name,Sex,Age,SibSp,Parch,Ticket,Fare,
    Cabin,Embarked
1,0,3,"Braund, Mr. Owen Harris",male,22,1,0,A/5 21171,7.25,,S
2,1,1,"Cumings, Mrs. John Bradley (Florence Briggs Thayer)",female
    ,38,1,0,PC 17599,71.2833,C85,C
3,1,3,"Heikkinen, Miss. Laina",female,26,0,0,STON/O2.
    3101282,7.925,,S
4,1,1,"Futrelle, Mrs. Jacques Heath (Lily May Peel)",female
    ,35,1,0,113803,53.1,C123,S
5,0,3,"Allen, Mr. William Henry",male,35,0,0,373450,8.05,,S
6,0,3,"Moran, Mr. James",male,,0,0,330877,8.4583,,Q
```

In the training data, the first row contains the column headings that describe the attributes, or features, for your predictions. The outcome is the second column, which is named *Survived*. As you can observe, several columns are not numerical in the data set. However, models must deal with numeric data. The training set columns are the following:

- Survived: categorical (1,0), 1 means lived, 0 means died.

- Pclass: ordinal (1,2,3), this is the class of the ticket; 1 is first class (most expensive) whereas 3 is 3rd class (least expensive).

- Name: textual

- Sex: categorical (m,f)

- Age: numeric, missing values

- Sibsp: numeric. The number of siblings/spouses aboard.

- Parch: numeric. The number of parents/children aboard.

- Ticket: textual, this is the ticket number.

10.2 Milestone 1: Wrangling the Data

- Fare: numeric, missing values

- Cabin: textual, this is the cabin number.

- Embarked: categorical (c,q,s), missing values. This is the port where the passenger got on the boat. C for Cherbourg, Q for Queenstown, S for Southampton

The training set contains numeric, categorical, and ordinal values. Categorical values are unordered and non-numeric, such as the *embarked* attribute. In other words, passengers departed from the ports in a specific order, but that order is not relevant for the model. On the other hand, the attribute *pclass* has an order and is therefore an ordinal. Because the passenger classes are numbers, we will treat *pclass* as numerical. We must also deal with missing values for the attributes *age*, *fare*, and *embarked*. As a result, we will attempt to interpolate these values. Interpolation means taking an average. However, we don't want to restrict the values that we average. For example, if we take the average fare of all three classes, we can better interpolate the fare when we know the class. The average fare for first class was 88 dollars; the average fare for third class was 13 dollars. Taking the average by class, rather than over all passengers, gives a more accurate result.

The output from my normalization process is shown here.

```
Master: Mean Age: 5.48 (Count: 76, survived: 0.5789473684210527,
    male.survived: 0.5789473684210527)
Mr.: Mean Age: 32.25215146299484 (Count: 915, survived:
    0.16174863387978142, male.survived: 0.16174863387978142)
Miss.: Mean Age: 21.795235849056603 (Count: 332, survived:
    0.7108433734939759, female.survived: 0.7108433734939759)
Mrs.: Mean Age: 36.91812865497076 (Count: 235, survived:
    0.7914893617021277, female.survived: 0.7914893617021277)
Military: Mean Age: 36.91812865497076 (Count: 10, survived: 0.4,
    male.survived: 0.4)
Clergy: Mean Age: 41.25 (Count: 12, survived: 0.0, male.survived:
    0.0)
Nobility: Mean Age: 41.166666666666664 (Count: 10, survived: 0.6,
    male.survived: 0.333333333333333, female.survived: 1.0)
Dr: Mean Age: 43.57142857142857 (Count: 13, survived:
    0.46153846153846156, male.survived: 0.36363636363636365,
    female.survived: 1.0)
```

```
Total known survival: Mean Age: 29.881137667304014 (Count: 891,
    survived: 0.3838383838383838, male.survived:
    0.18890814558058924, female.survived: 0.7420382165605095)
Embarked Queenstown: Mean Age: (Count: 77, survived:
    0.38961038961038963, male.survived: 0.07317073170731707,
    female.survived: 0.75)
Embarked Southampton: Mean Age: (Count: 644, survived:
    0.33695652173913043, male.survived: 0.1746031746031746, female
    .survived: 0.6896551724137931)
Embarked Cherbourg: Mean Age: (Count: 168, survived:
    0.5535714285714286, male.survived: 0.30526315789473685, female
    .survived: 0.8767123287671232)
Most common embarked: Mean Age: S
Mean Age Male: 30.58522796352584
Mean Age Female: 28.68708762886598
Mean Fair 1st Class: 87.5089916408668
Mean Fair 2st Class: 21.1791963898917
Mean Fair 3st Class: 13.302888700564969
```

The data provokes some interesting observations. Although the name field might seem unhelpful at first glance because it is purely textual, the prefixes, such as "Mr.," "Miss," "Ms.," "Master," "Col.," "Major," "Count," and "Rev.," could provide useful data for prediction. However, data wrangling is necessary because these values are locked away in the name text.

I classified the prefixes in the following way: "Master," "Mr.," "Miss," "Mrs.," "Military," "Nobility," "Doctor," and "Clergy." The first lines of the output show you the survival rates for each category.

The term "master" might be confusing in modern English. The Merriam-Webster on-line dictionary lists an archaic definition for it.

Master (2): a youth or boy too young to be called mister –used as a title

While this definition is outdated in 2014 English, it was commonly employed in 1912 English. For our purposes, it helps us determine the ages of Titanic passengers. In the data set, the average age for "master" was 5.48 years; the average age for "mister" was 32 years. The average age for nobility was 41 years.

10.2 Milestone 1: Wrangling the Data

Titles also seem to influence survival rates. Despite the young age of "master," only 58% of the boys on the ship survived. None of the clergy survived. On the other hand, all of the female nobles survived. Additionally, 40% of the male military, and 60% of the male nobility survived.

Lastly, the departure city also seems to affect the passengers' fates. Queenstown and Southampton both had survival rates around 30%, whereas 55% of the passengers who boarded at Cherbourg lived. Besides departure city, the listing shows other statistics that I calculated.

These values helped me to determine the appropriate data parts for prediction. Ultimately, the model can accept only numeric data. This input is the feature vector; the following points show the feature vector for Titanic:

- Age: The interpolated age normalized to -1 to 1.

- Sex-male: The gender normalized to -1 for female, 1 for male.

- Pclass: The passenger class [1-3] normalized to -1 to 1.

- Sibsp: Value from the original data set normalized to -1 to 1.

- Parch: Value from the original data set normalized to -1 to 1.

- Fare: The interpolated fare normalized to -1 to 1.

- Embarked-c: The value 1 if the passenger embarked from Cherbourg, -1 otherwise.

- Embarked-q: The value 1 if the passenger embarked from Queenstown, -1 otherwise.

- Embarked-s: The value 1 if the passenger embarked from Southampton, -1 otherwise.

- Name-mil: The value 1 if passenger had a military prefix, -1 otherwise.

- Name-nobility: The value 1 if passenger had a noble prefix, -1 otherwise.

- Name-Dr.: The value 1 if passenger had a doctor prefix, -1 otherwise.

- Name-clergy: The value 1 if passenger had a clergy prefix, -1 otherwise.

I experimented with several feature vectors and ultimately chose the ones that I just listed. Some prefixes were only for age interpolation while others were Boolean flags in the feature vector. I normalized every value between -1 and 1. The RBF neural network model works best with this input range. Normalizing categorical values to separate features is important. I normalized the three separate features for the three ports from which the passengers embarked. Because **pclass** is ordinal, a single feature is required.

10.3 Milestone 2: Build a Model

The Titanic data set can accommodate many models. Of course, some models perform better for certain data sets than others. Simple decision trees were reported to achieve scores in the upper 70's. Hybrid approaches, involving gradient boosting machines (GBM), were popular among competitors and received scores in the lower 80's. The example in the book utilizes an RBF neural network because I presented only this model.

To build the model, cross-validation gives me a good estimate of my actual Kaggle score for a particular model. Cross-validation is a statistical technique that allows me to work with a single set of data for both training and validation. Cross-validation attempts to combat overfitting by using different parts of the data set for training and validation. To understand overfitting, consider a student preparing to take a certification exam. To help the student prepare, the certification provider offers a practice exam that the student repeatedly takes until he achieves a passing grade. Despite the extensive work with the practice exam, the student's chances of success on the real certification exam are not necessarily guaranteed.

In all likelihood, the student will not do well on the real exam. The student has undoubtedly memorized the exam after several attempts; he has not really learned the material in spite of the false hope generated by many retries at the same practice exam. The same issue can occur with a model. After many training runs with the Titanic data, our model might begin to memorize rather than learn. At some point, we may even achieve a 100% training score, which does not mean that we will get a 100% score on Kaggle. Consequently, we need a way to predict our actual Kaggle score.

10.3 Milestone 2: Build a Model

Overfitting typically occurs on an RBF network when training has progressed for too long. Extremely lengthy training runs will continue to improve the training score of the RBF indefinitely as the score slowly approaches 100%. Because these sessions encourage an RBF network to memorize, we need a process that stops training early before memorization begins.

To implement early stopping, we divide the data into a training portion and a validation portion. As its name implies, the training data is only for training. Once every training iteration has ended, the model is evaluated with the validation data. Training stops once the validation score ceases to improve. Keep in mind that the validation data only evaluates when to stop; it does not improve the training score. The final evaluation score will give us a reasonably good estimate of our Kaggle score.

We can do better than a single validation and training partition. Cross-validation breaks the training set into folds. I will utilize five folds and train five models over five cycles for this example. Because we use five folds, we will have five cycles. During each cycle, one of the folds plays the role of validation, and the others are combined into a training set. Figure 10.3 shows this process.

Figure 10.3: Cross-Validation

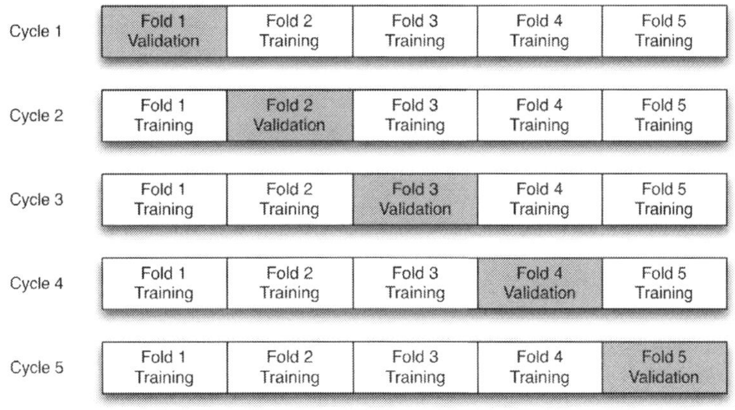

During each training cycle, we build a separate model and stop training once the network no longer improvises its score with the validation fold. Particle swarm optimization (PSO) trains the model. Once we stop, the average validation score over all cycles gives us an even better estimate of our future Kaggle score.

The ultimate goal is to achieve a good score on data that the neural network has never seen. As a result, the validation set provides a good test for the network. We stop once the validation score is no longer improving during training.

You can see the complete training process in the listing below.

```
Cross validation fold #1/5
Fold #1, Iteration #1: training correct: 0.6067415730337079,
    validation correct: 0.6536312849162011, no improvement: 0
Fold #1, Iteration #2: training correct: 0.6067415730337079,
    validation correct: 0.6536312849162011, no improvement: 1
Fold #1, Iteration #3: training correct: 0.6067415730337079,
    validation correct: 0.6536312849162011, no improvement: 2
...
Fold #1, Iteration #28: training correct: 0.6067415730337079,
    validation correct: 0.6536312849162011, no improvement: 27
Fold #1, Iteration #29: training correct: 0.6067415730337079,
    validation correct: 0.6536312849162011, no improvement: 28
Fold #1, Iteration #30: training correct: 0.6123595505617978,
    validation correct: 0.659217877094972, no improvement: 0
Fold #1, Iteration #31: training correct: 0.6853932584269663,
    validation correct: 0.7541899441340782, no improvement: 0
Fold #1, Iteration #32: training correct: 0.6853932584269663,
    validation correct: 0.7541899441340782, no improvement: 1
...
Fold #1, Iteration #239: training correct: 0.8047752808988764,
    validation correct: 0.8491620111731844, no improvement: 100
Fold #1, Iteration #240: training correct: 0.8047752808988764,
    validation correct: 0.8491620111731844, no improvement: 101
Cross validation fold #2/5
Fold #2, Iteration #1: training correct: 0.6171107994389902,
    validation correct: 0.6123595505617978, no improvement: 0
...
Fold #2, Iteration #165: training correct: 0.8050490883590463,
    validation correct: 0.8426966292134831, no improvement: 101
Cross validation fold #3/5
Fold #3, Iteration #1: training correct: 0.6143057503506312,
    validation correct: 0.6235955056179775, no improvement: 0
...
Fold #3, Iteration #121: training correct: 0.8176718092566619,
```

```
    validation correct: 0.797752808988764, no improvement: 101
Cross validation fold #4/5
Fold #4, Iteration #1: training correct: 0.6129032258064516,
    validation correct: 0.6292134831460674, no improvement: 0
...
Fold #4, Iteration #145: training correct: 0.8260869565217391,
    validation correct: 0.7528089887640449, no improvement: 101
Cross validation fold #5/5
Fold #5, Iteration #1: training correct: 0.6297335203366059,
    validation correct: 0.5617977528089888, no improvement: 0
...
Fold #5, Iteration #165: training correct: 0.8218793828892006,
    validation correct: 0.7752808988764045, no improvement: 101
Cross-validation summary:
Fold #1: 0.8547486033519553
Fold #2: 0.8426966292134831
Fold #3: 0.8089887640449438
Fold #4: 0.7528089887640449
Fold #5: 0.7752808988764045
Final, cross-validated score:0.8069047768501664
```

The listing demonstrates that training progressed through all 5 folds. Both the training and validation scores are shown. However, our interest is solely in the validation score. Once it failed to improve for 100 iterations, we stopped the training. At the end of the process, we assume that our Kaggle score will approximate the average of the scores from the 5 folds. Although we can't predict our exact Kaggle score, this process provides a rough estimate.

10.4 Milestone 3: Submit a Test Response

Now we can take the best model from the second milestone and submit it to Kaggle. As a result, we process the data provided in the Kaggle test data set. The Kaggle test data set does not include the outcomes. The best model must generate those outcomes and generate a submission file. Listing 10.2 shows the simple submission file.

Listing 10.2: Kaggle Titanic Submission File

```
"PassengerId","Survived"
"892","0"
"893","0"
"894","0"
"895","0"
"896","0"
"897","0"
"898","1"
"899","0"
"900","1"
...
```

The above data is essentially an answer sheet for an exam because it contains only the passenger number and our prediction. To generate the submission file, we simply pass every item in the test set through our model. The actual test set, provided by Kaggle, contains all the passenger attributes; however, we need to report only the passenger identification and outcome.

Once you submit the file to Kaggle, you receive an official score that details the number of correct responses you obtained. The RBF neural network scores 79%, as seen in Figure 10.4.

Figure 10.4: A Kaggle Submission and Score

This score is not too far from the cross-validated estimate of 80%. Further experimentation might improve the score. For example, I did nothing with the ticket identification. Extracting cabin location from this field and obtaining another attribute for the model might be possible for future tests. I got 79% with nine submissions. Ultimately, Kaggle requires a lot of trial and error; succeeding in a Kaggle competition might involve hundreds of submissions.

10.5 Chapter Summary

I discussed how to apply some of the techniques from earlier chapters to data science. Prediction is one of the primary applications for data science. Furthermore, artificial intelligence is a central component of this active field.

This chapter introduced the Titanic problem that serves as the tutorial competition in Kaggle. The goal is to create a model that can predict survival rates of Titanic passengers based on attributes in a data set. Several challenges are present in the competition. For example, most data contain unpredictable outliers. Overfitting occurs when the model attempts to memorize these outliers, and this negatively impacts the model's ability to predict mainstream data. As a result, cross-validation can prevent overfitting and allows competitors to gain a realistic estimate of their Kaggle score.

Nature-inspired algorithms are an area of active research in the field of artificial intelligence. I introduced you to many of these algorithms. Cooperative and competitive populations optimize solutions to a score function. Cellular automata can produce very complex patterns with a simple set of rules. Artificial life attempts to recreate aspects of nature for entertainment or simulation purposes. Flocks of birds and ant colonies can teach us to optimize and improve processes. Particle swarm optimization can fit models, such as the RBF neural network, to data and predict whether a passenger survived the Titanic disaster.

If you are interested in learning more about artificial intelligence, the next book in this series will focus on neural network models, including both traditional neural networks as well as deep belief neural networks (DBNN). Some of the algorithms examined in this book will be applied to evolve NEAT and HyperNEAT neural networks. Although neural networks were originally based on the human brain, they now refer to nearly any AI model using connections. These models will be the topic of the next book.

Appendix A

Examples

- Downloading Examples
- Structure of Example Download
- Keeping Updated

A.1 Artificial Intelligence for Humans

These examples are part of a series of books that is currently under development. Check the website to see which volumes have been completed and are available.

http://www.heatonresearch.com/aifh

The following volumes are planned for this series:

- Volume 0: Introduction to the Math of AI
- Volume 1: Fundamental Algorithms
- Volume 2: Nature-Inspired Algorithms
- Volume 3: Deep Belief and Neural Networks

A.2 Staying Up to Date

This appendix describes how to obtain the *Artificial Intelligence for Humans* (AIFH) book series examples.

This area is probably the most dynamic of the book. Computer languages are always changing and adding new versions. I will update the examples as it becomes necessary. There are also bugs and corrections. As a result, make sure that you are always using the latest version of the book examples.

Because this area is so dynamic, this file may become outdated. You can always find the latest version at the following location:

https://github.com/jeffheaton/aifh

A.3 Obtaining the Examples

I provide the book's examples in many programming languages. Core example packs exist for Java, C#, C/C++, Python and R for most volumes. Volume 2, as of publication, includes Java, C#, Python and Scala. Other languages may have been added since publication. The community may have added other languages as well. All examples can be found at the GitHub repository.

https://github.com/jeffheaton/aifh

You have your choice of two different ways to download the examples.

A.3.1 Download ZIP File

Github provides an icon that allows you to simply download a ZIP file that contains all of the example code for the series. A single ZIP file contains all of the examples for the series. As a result, I frequently update the contents of this ZIP. If you are starting a new volume, it is important that you verify that you have the latest copy. You can perform the download from the following URL:

A.3 Obtaining the Examples

https://github.com/jeffheaton/aifh

You can see the download link in Figure A.1.

Figure A.1: GitHub

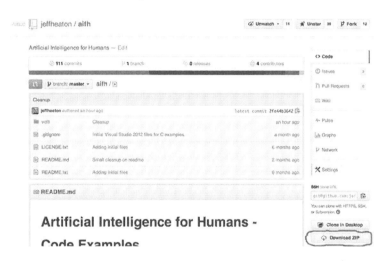

A.3.2 Clone the Git Repository

You can obtain all the examples with the source control program **git** if it is installed on your system. The following command clones the examples to your computer: (Cloning simply refers to the process of copying the example files.)

```
git clone https://github.com/jeffheaton/aifh.git
```

You can also pull the latest updates with the following command:

```
git pull
```

If you would like an introduction to **git,** refer to the following URL:

http://git-scm.com/docs/gittutorial

A.4 Example Contents

The entire *Artificial Intelligence for Humans* series is contained in one download that is a zip file.

Once you open the examples file, you will see the contents in Figure A.2.

Figure A.2: Examples Download

The license file describes the license for the book examples. All of the examples for this series are released under the Apache v2.0 license, a free and open-source software (FOSS) license. In other words, I do retain a copyright to the files. However, you can freely reuse these files in both commercial and non-commercial projects without further permission.

While the book source code is provided free, the book text is not provided free. These books are commercial products that I sell through a variety of channels. Consequently, you may not redistribute the actual books. This restriction includes the PDF, MOBI, EPUB and any other format of the book. However, I provide all books in DRM-free form. I appreciate your support of this policy because it contributes to the future growth of these books.

The download also includes two README files. The README.md is a "markdown" file that contains images and formatting. The README.txt is plain text. Both files contain the same information. For more information on MD files, refer to the following URL:

https://help.github.com/articles/github-flavored-markdown

You will find README files in several folders of the book's examples. The

A.4 Example Contents

README file in the examples root (seen above) has information about the book series.

You will also notice the individual volume folders in the download. These are named vol1, vol2, etc. You may not see all of the volumes in the download because I have not yet written them. All of the volumes have the same format. For example, if you open Volume 1, you will see the contents listed in Figure A.3. Other volumes will have a similar layout, depending on the languages that are added.

Figure A.3: Inside Volume 1

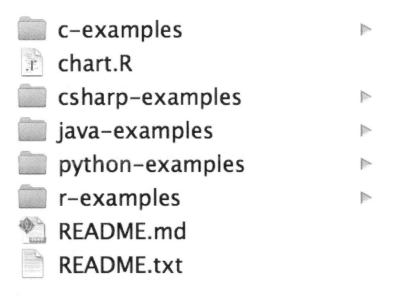

Again, you see the two README files that contain information unique to this particular volume. The most important information in the volume level README files is the current status of the examples. The community often contributes example packs. As a result, some of the example packs may not be complete. The README for the volume will let you know this important information. The volume README also contains the FAQ for a volume.

You should also see a file named "charts.RMD". This file contains the R markdown source code that created many charts in the book. The R programming language produced nearly all the graphs and charts in the book. The file ultimately allows you to see the equations behind the pictures. Nevertheless, I do not translate this file to other programming languages. I utilize R simply for the production of the book. If I had used another language, like Python, to produce some of the charts, you would see a "charts.py" along with the R code.

Additionally, the volume has examples for C, C#, Java, Python, and R. I also want to include complete examples for these core languages. However, you may see that I add other languages. So, always check the README file for the latest information on language translations.

Figure A.4 shows the contents of a typical language pack.

Figure A.4: The Java Language Pack

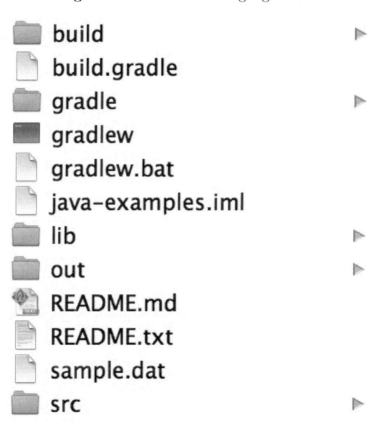

Pay attention to the README files. The README files in a language folder are important because you will find information about the Java examples. If you have difficulty using the book's examples with a particular language, the README file should be your first step to solving the problem. The other files in the above image are all unique to Java. The README file describes these files in much greater detail.

A.5 Contributing to the Project

If you would like to translate the examples to a new language or if you have found an error in the book, you can help. Fork the project and push a commit revision to GitHub. I will credit you among the growing number of contributors.

The process begins with a fork. You create an account on GitHub and fork the AIFH project. This step creates a new project that has a copy of the AIFH files. You will then clone your new project through GitHub. Once you make your changes, you submit a "pull request." When I receive this request, I will evaluate your changes/additions and merge it with the main project.

You can find a more detailed article on contributing through GitHub at this URL:

https://help.github.com/articles/fork-a-repo

References

This section lists the reference materials for this book.

Baker, J. E. (1987). Reducing Bias and Inefficiency in the Selection Algorithm. *Genetic algorithms and their applications: proceedings of the second International Conference on Genetic Algorithms* : July 28-31, 1987 at the Massachusetts Institute of Technology, Cambridge, MA (pp. 14-21). Hillsdale, N.J.: L. Erlbaum Associates.

Balack, T. (1996). *Evolutionary algorithms in theory and practice evolution strategies, evolutionary programming, genetic algorithms.* New York: Oxford University Press.

Blum, C., & Socha, K. (2005). *Training feed-forward neural networks with ant colony optimization: An application to pattern classification. Training feed-forward neural networks with ant colony optimization*: An application to pattern classification. Retrieved July 27, 2014, from http://www.computer.org/csdl/proceedings/his/2005/2457/00/24570233-abs.html

Conway, D. (2013). The Data Science Venn Diagram. *Drew Conway BLOG.* Retrieved July 27, 2014, from http://drewconway.com/zia/2013/3/26/the-data-science-venn-diagram

Conway, J. (1970, October). Mathematical Games- The fantastic combinations of John Conway's new solitaire game "life". *Scientific American, 223,* 120-123.

Cook, O. F. (1906). Factors Of Species-Formation. *Science*, 23(587), 506-507.

Deb, K., Pratap, A., & Agarwal, S. (2002). A fast and elitist multiobjective genetic algorithm: NSGA-II. *IEEE Transactions on Evolutionary Computation*, 6(2), 182 - 197.

Dorigo, M. (2007). Ant colony optimization. *Scholarpedia*, 2(3), 1461.

Hartmanis, J. (1982). Computers and Intractability: A Guide to the Theory of NP-Completeness (Michael R. Garey and David S. Johnson). *SIAM Review*, 24(1), 90.

Heaton, J. (2014). Using an evolutionary algorithm to create a cellular automata. *CodeProject*. Retrieved July 27, 2014, from http://www.codeproject.com/Articles/730362/Using-an-evolutionary-algorithm-to-create-a-cellul

HoÌLlldobler, B., & Wilson, E. O. (1990). The ants. Cambridge, Mass.: *Belknap Press of Harvard University Press*.

Kaufman, L., & Rousseeuw, P. (2010). Computational Complexity between K-Means and K-Medoids Clustering Algorithms for Normal and Uniform Distributions of Data Points. *Journal of Computer Science*, 6(3), 363-368.

Kennedy, J. (1999). Minds and Cultures: Particle Swarm Implications For Beings in Sociocognitive Space. *Adaptive Behavior*, 7(3-4), 269-287.

Koza, J. R. (1992). Genetic programming: on the programming of computers by means of natural selection. Cambridge, Mass.: *MIT Press*.

Miller, B. L., & Goldberg, D. E. (1995). Genetic Algorithms, Tournament Selection, and the Effects of Noise. *Complex Systems*, 9, 193-212.

Mitchell, M. (1996). An introduction to genetic algorithms. Cambridge, Mass.: *MIT Press*.

MÃijhlenbein, H., & Schlierkamp-Voosen, D. (1993). Predictive Models for the Breeder Genetic Algorithm I. Continuous Parameter Optimization. *Evolutionary Computation*, 1(1), 25-49.

Poli, R., & Langdon, W. B. (2008). A field guide to genetic programming. S.I.: *[Lulu Press], lulu.com*.

Reynolds, C. W. (1987). Flocks, Herds And Schools: A Distributed Behavioral Model. *ACM SIGGRAPH Computer Graphics*, 21(4), 25-34.

Snell, D. (2013, December). Genetic Algorithms- "Useful, Fun and Easy!. *Forecasting* & Futurism Newsletter, 6, 7-15.

Stanley, K., D'Ambrosio, D., & Gauci, J. (2009). A Hypercube-Based Indirect Encoding for Evolving Large-Scale Neural Networks. *Artificial Life journal*, 15(2), 1-10.

Vitter, J. S. (1985). Random sampling with a reservoir. *ACM Transactions On Mathematical Software*, 11(1), 37-57.

Wolfram, S. (2002). A new kind of science. Champaign, IL: *Wolfram Media*.

Index

algorithm, xvii, xix, xxv–xxvii, xxxiv, xxxvi, xxxviii, 2–13, 15–17, 19, 20, 23–27, 29, 31, 32, 36–38, 41, 42, 44–47, 49, 51–54, 56, 59, 65, 68, 69, 71–77, 79, 80, 82, 83, 85, 87–94, 97–99, 101–103, 105, 107, 109, 111–114, 118, 120, 123–126, 129, 130, 141, 142, 145, 147–149, 151, 164, 166, 169, 183

ant, iv–vii, xviii, xix, xxiv, xxv, xxvii, xxx, xxxi, xxxiv, xxxvi–xxxviii, 5, 6, 10, 14, 15, 18, 19, 26–29, 32, 34, 36, 42, 44–46, 49, 60, 65, 67, 69, 74–76, 78, 82, 84, 85, 87–90, 99–102, 107, 109–126, 130, 132, 141, 146–149, 151–153, 155–167, 169–171, 173, 175, 178, 183, 186, 189–191

ant colony optimization, xix, 5, 49, 107, 164

arrays, xxvi, xxxiii, 26, 28, 29, 32, 33, 36, 56, 74, 85, 90, 91

artificial intelligence, xvii, xxi, xxii, xxv, 52, 169, 183

asexual reproduction, 27, 77

backer, xxviii, 130, 151

best score, 5, 11, 12, 19, 20, 37, 38, 47, 51, 102, 105

best solution, xxvi, 5, 6, 11, 13, 14, 27, 44, 48, 102

beta, 112, 115

better solution, xxvi, 2, 20, 28, 56

categorical, 26–29, 32, 38, 45, 47, 175, 178

centroid, 90, 91

children, 4, 5, 11, 29, 32, 33, 38, 68, 75, 85, 173

chosen, xxxvi, 2, 3, 9, 12, 16, 17, 19, 20, 25, 71, 72, 79, 114, 115, 118, 123

cities, 2, 26, 42–48, 102, 103, 111, 112

clustering, 89, 90

cockatiel, 55

coefficient, xxxiv, xxxvi–xxxviii, 54, 124

competition, xxvii, 4, 171–173, 182, 183

competitive population, 4, 5, 7, 20, 23, 25, 97, 127, 183

computer science, xviii, xxi, 45, 59, 74, 114, 171

constant pool, 65, 69

constants, 65, 67, 84, 100, 101, 112, 141, 146, 147

contender, 12, 171

converge, 83, 94, 100, 112, 124, 137, 138, 140–143
cooperative population, 5, 7, 20, 97, 107, 126
crossover, xxvi, 14, 20, 24–27, 31–34, 36–38, 41, 45, 47, 49, 51, 56, 74, 79, 83–85, 87–89, 94, 149

data set, xxvii, xxx, xxxi, xxxiii, xxxiv, xxxvi, xxxvii, 8, 49–52, 56, 68, 81, 82, 93, 105, 107, 120, 125, 171–174, 176, 178, 181, 183
default, 25, 89, 99, 119, 155
dimensions, xxix–xxxi, xxxiv, xxxv, 101, 103, 149
discrete, 26, 42, 45, 47, 109, 111, 112, 114, 120, 126, 127
discrete learning, 42, 111
distributed computing, 7, 10, 20

elitism , 5, 11, 25, 49
elitism count, 49
evaporation, 110, 112, 118, 119, 124
evolutionary, xxvi, 3, 4, 6, 8, 11, 12, 15, 20, 23–27, 31, 32, 36–38, 41, 68, 85, 87, 89, 93, 141, 151, 159, 165, 166
evolutionary algorithm, xxvi, 3, 4, 6, 8, 11, 15, 20, 23–27, 31, 32, 36–38, 41, 68, 85, 87, 89, 93, 141, 151, 166

fitness function, 8, 24
fixed-length, xxvi, 26, 41, 47, 55, 56, 74, 85, 88, 90, 91, 94, 167
fixed-length array, xxvi, 26, 41, 55, 56, 74, 85, 90, 91

flock, xxvi, 2, 98, 99, 101, 102, 107
flocking, 98, 99, 101, 102, 107
function, xxxiii–xxxviii, 8, 14, 24–26, 29, 35, 41, 44–47, 50, 51, 54, 55, 60–64, 66, 67, 71, 72, 75, 77, 79, 83, 85, 91, 101, 116–118, 120–123, 125, 126, 142, 166, 183

generation, xxv, xxvi, 2, 4–6, 9, 11–13, 19, 20, 23–25, 27, 37, 38, 48, 51, 54, 56, 69, 84, 89, 90, 93, 94, 97, 130, 152, 165
generations, xxv, 2, 4, 5, 19, 24, 37, 56, 93, 94, 97, 152, 165
genetic algorithm, xvii, xix, xxvii, 5, 25, 41, 42, 44–47, 49, 51, 52, 54, 56, 59, 77, 83, 85, 88, 91–94, 105, 109, 120, 125, 126, 142, 145, 149, 164
genetic programming, 5, 26, 56, 59, 65, 68, 69, 71, 81–83, 91, 92, 94
genetic programs, 1, 77, 84
genome, xxv, xxvi, 45, 46, 54, 55, 83, 84, 88–94, 162
genotype, 6
greedy, 6
groups, xxvi, 3, 31, 65

hyper-parameters, 50, 51, 68, 69

individual, xxvi, xxxi, xxxv, 3–5, 7, 8, 11, 14–20, 23, 25, 31, 36–38, 68, 76, 87, 90, 97, 98, 107, 122, 129, 146, 160, 172, 173, 189

INDEX

initial population, 4, 45, 69, 73
initialization, 69, 71, 73
iris, xxvi, xxx, xxxi, xxxiii, xxxiv, xxxvi–xxxviii, 42, 49–52, 56, 68, 93, 105, 107, 125
iris data, xxx, xxxi, xxxiii, xxxiv, xxxvi, 49–52, 56, 68, 93, 105, 107, 125
iris species, xxvi, xxxi, xxxiii, xxxvii, xxxviii, 49
island, 7
iterations, 4, 11, 20, 44, 48, 51, 97, 106, 126, 135, 138, 141, 181
iterative, 6, 43, 45

k-means, 90, 91

mate, v, vi, xxiii, xxiv, xxxi, xxxvi, xxxviii, 1, 5, 7, 31, 36, 37, 48, 76, 85, 102, 123, 126, 129, 135–137, 142, 145, 148, 149, 151, 157, 159, 162, 167, 177–183, 190, 193
mathematical, xxii, xxiv, 60, 85, 148
max, xxxiv, xxxv, 4, 6, 8, 69, 71, 73, 83, 102, 105, 111, 132, 155, 161, 167
maximization, 102
maximize, 6, 8, 105, 111, 167
measurements, xxvi, xxx, xxxiii, 49, 68
members, xxv, xxvi, 2–6, 8, 12, 14, 17, 19, 20, 37, 38, 45, 87–90, 98
minimization, 102
model, xxvi, xxvii, xxxi, xxxiii–xxxv, xxxvii, xxxviii, 1, 2, 8, 12, 13, 36, 49–51, 69, 82, 100–102, 105, 107, 120, 123–126, 151, 164, 169, 171–175, 177–183
model parameters, 102, 105
models, xxxiii, 1, 2, 8, 36, 49, 82, 100, 171, 174, 178, 179, 183
monogamy , 37
mosaic, 54–56
multiplication, 60–62, 65, 67
mutate, 26, 31, 34, 84, 148
mutation, 20, 24–31, 36–38, 41, 45–47, 49, 51, 56, 74, 77, 83–85, 149
mutation percent, 25

nature-inspired, xxvii, 6, 7, 27, 31, 87, 88, 107, 169
neural, xix, xxiv, xxv, xxx, xxxvii, 1, 6, 42, 101, 105–107, 120, 123, 125, 178, 180, 182, 183
neural network, xix, xxiv, xxv, xxx, xxxvii, 1, 6, 42, 101, 105–107, 120, 123, 125, 178, 180, 182, 183
next generation, xxvi, 4, 5, 9, 11, 20, 23, 25, 27, 37, 38, 56, 93, 130
node, xxxvii, xxxviii, 64–69, 71–77, 84, 85, 92, 113–118
non-repeating, 33, 34, 47
numbers, xxx, xxxii, xxxiii, 16, 26, 33, 34, 45, 65, 100, 101, 120, 121, 123, 126, 132, 141, 146, 149, 175
numeric, xxx, xxxi, xxxiii, xxxv, xxxviii, 8, 20, 26–29, 32, 38, 42, 49, 65, 69, 81, 111, 141, 146, 163, 174, 175, 177
numerical, xxx, 26, 27, 38, 174, 175

offspring, xxvi, 4, 27, 28, 30, 31, 33, 34, 36–38, 77, 80, 84, 85, 87, 88, 93, 94, 148

opcode, 62, 67–69, 71, 72

operators, 12, 24, 26, 36, 38, 41, 45, 47, 60, 61, 65, 74, 85

optimal, xxv–xxvii, 27, 31, 42, 47, 49, 51, 84, 97, 101, 107, 111, 113, 126

optimization, xix, xxxviii, 5, 20, 49, 94, 101, 105, 107, 109, 120, 125, 126, 149, 164, 180, 183

organism, xxv, xxvi, 2, 6, 7, 27, 31, 38, 87, 88, 94, 166

outputs, xxxvii, xxxviii, 8

parallel, 7, 10, 12, 13, 16, 19, 20

parameter vector, xxxiv, xxxvi, 51, 123

parent, 4, 5, 11, 13–15, 20, 23, 25, 27–34, 36, 38, 61, 64, 77–80, 84, 85, 87, 93, 94, 99, 148, 155

particle, xix, xxvi, 5, 20, 49, 94, 99–103, 105, 107, 109, 120, 125, 126, 138, 139, 164

particle swarm optimization, xix, 5, 20, 49, 94, 101, 107, 109, 120, 125, 126, 164

paths, xxv, 43, 44, 46, 47, 107, 109–111, 118, 126

perturb, 29–31

perturb mutation, 29, 30

phenotype, 6

pheromone, xxvii, 107, 109, 110, 113–115, 117–120, 124, 126

plants, xxvii, 27, 87, 149, 151, 153, 159, 164, 167

population, xxvi, 2–11, 13, 14, 16–20, 23, 25, 26, 37, 38, 41, 45–47, 49, 56, 68, 69, 73, 75, 76, 89–91, 93, 97, 102, 107, 122, 123, 126, 127, 164, 183

population size , 4, 14, 18, 25

potential solution, xxv, xxvi, 3–9, 20, 25–27, 45, 51

pow, 60, 62, 103, 115, 118, 132

probabilities, 101, 115–117

probability, 17, 19, 73, 88, 94, 109, 114–117, 120, 121, 126, 170

programmer, xviii, xxv, xxvii, xxx, 32, 45, 47, 49, 50, 60, 98, 99, 121, 126, 141, 146

programming language, xviii, xxii, 45, 54, 61, 65, 148, 186, 190

programs, v, vii, xxiii, xxiv, xxvi, xxvii, 1, 44, 56, 59, 60, 77, 84, 85, 135, 141, 170

proportionate, 15–17, 19, 20

pseudocode, xviii, xxii, xxxiii, 10, 16, 18, 28, 30, 31, 33, 34, 69, 71, 74, 76, 77, 79, 104, 116, 124, 156, 166

radial-basis function, xxxiii–xxxvi

random, xxxiv, 1, 3, 4, 8, 11, 12, 17, 18, 20, 25, 27–33, 45, 47, 48, 65, 68, 69, 71, 73–79, 94, 100, 103, 105, 109, 111, 114, 115, 117, 120–123, 130, 137, 143, 146, 148, 149

random forests, 1

random node, 69, 75, 77, 117

random number, 17, 18, 31, 74–76, 100, 121–123, 130, 146, 149
random point, 18, 77–79
randomly, 3, 4, 20, 28, 29, 32, 47, 74, 76, 77, 94, 109, 111, 143
regression, xxxiii, xxxviii, 5, 81
represents, xxxvi, xxxvii, 6, 26, 27, 51, 61, 67, 81, 82, 90, 111, 113, 115, 118, 159, 164
reservoir, 76, 77
root node, 64, 66, 69, 71, 72, 75, 77
roulette wheel, 15, 20, 123
rounds, 11, 12, 14, 15
rules, xxvii, 46, 60, 61, 99, 107, 126, 127, 129, 131–135, 137, 141, 149, 151, 183

salesman, xxvi, 42, 44, 46, 47, 52, 56, 111, 114, 126
sample, xxxi, 3, 9, 17, 44, 77, 82, 120, 121, 123, 124
sampling, 3, 9, 17–20, 75, 76, 120, 123
scores, 2, 5, 6, 16, 17, 19, 20, 37, 45, 93, 112, 122, 166, 172, 178, 181, 182
scoring, 2, 5, 11, 14, 19, 25, 37, 41, 45, 47, 54–56, 83, 123, 142, 166
scoring function, 25, 41, 45, 47, 54, 55, 83, 142, 166
search space, xxxi, 101, 102
selection, 2–5, 9–20, 23, 24, 37, 41, 47, 72, 75, 76, 84, 93, 114–116, 121
selection algorithm, 9–11, 16, 19, 20, 37
selection process, 2, 9, 16, 23, 76

sexual reproduction, 27, 31, 38, 77
shortest, 2, 42, 43, 111, 114
shuffle, 27, 28, 34, 47
shuffle mutation, 27, 28, 47
simple rules, xxvii, 99, 107, 127, 141
solution, xviii, xxv–xxvii, 1–9, 11, 13, 14, 20, 24–31, 33, 36, 38, 41, 44, 45, 47, 48, 50, 51, 56, 59, 65, 76, 83–85, 87, 94, 97, 102, 107, 111, 112, 120, 122, 123, 127, 151, 183
solution array, xxvi, 27–29, 36, 38, 59
sorted, 9, 10, 19, 20
speciation, xxvi, 36, 41, 87–94
speciation threshold, 88, 89, 92, 94
species, xxvi, xxx, xxxi, xxxiii, xxxvii, xxxviii, 2, 3, 42, 49, 52, 85, 87–94
splice crossover, 32–34, 47
stagnation, 19, 83
statistics, xviii, xxx, 3, 123, 169, 170, 177
stochastic universal sampling, 17–19
summation, xxxvi–xxxviii, 115, 123
support vector machines, 1, 101
swarm, xix, xxvi, 5, 20, 25, 49, 94, 98, 101, 107, 109, 120, 125, 126, 164, 180, 183
swarm optimization, xix, 5, 20, 49, 94, 101, 107, 109, 120, 125, 126, 164, 180, 183
synchronization , 7

terminal, 65, 67, 71, 72
threshold speciation, 88–91, 93
top score, 5, 37

tournament selection, 11, 13, 14, 19
trails, xxvii, 107, 109, 112, 113, 117–119, 126
training parameters, 49, 73, 88, 112
training setting, 5, 11, 14, 32, 49, 68, 69, 112, 113
traits, xxvi, 20, 27, 38, 87
traveling salesman problem, xxvi, 42, 44, 46, 52, 56, 111, 114, 126
traversal, 74, 75, 77
tree initialization, 69, 71
trees, xxv, xxvi, 36, 59, 69, 74, 79, 81, 85, 92, 94, 178
truncation selection, 9–11, 16
two-dimensional, xxx, xxxii, 101

universal sampling, 17–20

values, xxxv, xxxviii, 5, 25, 26, 28, 38, 42, 44, 63, 65, 69, 81, 82, 99, 102–104, 111, 112, 118, 120, 122–124, 126, 129–132, 146–148, 156, 159, 162, 175–178
vector, xxix–xxxvi, xxxviii, 1, 41, 49, 51, 54, 101–103, 105, 107, 116, 120, 122, 123, 126, 141, 142, 144, 146–148, 156, 158–165, 167, 177, 178
velocity, 102, 103, 105
visiting, 75, 76, 111, 114, 118

weights, xxx, xxxiv, xxxvii, 42, 101, 102, 120, 122
width, xxxi, xxxvii, 113, 120, 159
words, xxx, xxxii, xxxiii, 25, 27, 31, 46, 52–54, 65, 69, 89–91, 97, 99, 132, 155, 170, 171, 173, 175, 188
world population, 75, 76

Made in the USA
Middletown, DE
17 October 2014